VIBRANT ANDALUSIA

VIBRANT ANDALUSIA

The Spice of Life in Southern Spain

Ana Ruiz

Algora Publishing
New York

ISBN-13: 978-0-87586-539-3 (trade paper)
ISBN-13: 978-0-87586-540-9 (hard cover)
ISBN-13: 978-0-87586-541-6 (ebook)

Library of Congress Cataloging-in-Publication Data —

Ruiz, Ana, 1960-
  Vibrant Andalusia : Moorish culture in southern Spain / Ana Ruiz.
    p. cm.
  Includes bibliographical references and index.
    ISBN 978-0-87586-539-3 (trade paper : alk. paper) — ISBN 978-0-87586-540-9 (hard
cover: alk. paper) — ISBN 978-0-87586-541-6 (ebook) 1. Andalusia (Spain)—Civilization.
I. Title.

  DP302.A467R65 2007
  946'.802—dc22
                                2007003859

Front Cover: Alcaizería in Granada

Printed in the United States

To my Andalusian, Basque, and Castilian family.

ACKNOWLEDGMENTS

I wish to acknowledge and thank the following people and organizations for their valuable contributions:

• Mª Carmen Millán Ráfales, Jefa del Dpto. and Natalia Cobo at Biblioteca del Centro de Documentación de Música y Danza (Casa de Castril), Granada.

• Mª Helena Rosales Varo, Biblioteca de Andalucía, Centro de Documentación Musical de Andalucía, Granada.

• Miriam Font at Escuela de Estudios Arabes (Casa de Chapiz), Granada.

• Centro de Documentación de Música y Danza, Madrid.

All of the photographs were taken by the author unless otherwise indicated. Lyrics and other translations are the author's. I wish to thank my father Manuel Ruiz for the artwork, my mother Isabel Ruiz for her literary knowledge, and Algora Publishing for supporting my work once again.

Ana Ruiz
Montreal, 2007

TABLE OF CONTENTS

FOREWORD

During various trips to my homeland of Spain, I have had the pleasure of visiting its southern region of Andalusia many times. The moment I stood before the commanding statue of its founder *Abd al-Rahman* in the coastal town of Almuñécar in Granada, I became most intrigued, and set out to research the history of this important figure and the land he founded. The result is several years of research and observations that I wish to share with the curious reader and inquisitive traveler.

My goal is provide an introduction to the history and culture of Moorish Spain, the arrival and influence of the Gypsies, and the origins and development of Flamenco, and to explore the etymology of numerous Arabisms that add color to the Spanish language. I hope this primer will inspire further reading as a myriad of detailed and academic works on these subjects are available for those who wish to explore more deeply this great land the Moors named *al-Andalus*.

1. EARLY SETTLERS

Vestiges of prehistoric man's daily life have been discovered throughout the Iberian Peninsula, revealing habitation here since the early Stone Age. Some of the oldest human bone fragments discovered in Europe were excavated in Spain. Remains found in the Cueva Mayor of the Atapuerca hills in the north, believed to belong to our earliest known ancestors, have been dated to one million years ago. The prehistoric caves of Nerja in the southern province of Málaga were discovered by five local boys in the late 1950s. Skeletal remains prove that man lived here over 20,000 years ago.

By far the most famous work of Paleolithic art in the Iberian Peninsula is the painted ceiling of the Altamira Caves in northern Spain. The cave was found by chance in 1868, and it wasn't until eleven years later that a little girl named Maria first noticed the paintings. Dubbed the "Sistine Chapel of Paleolithic Art," these prehistoric murals are at least 12,000 years old. They display lifelike hunting scenes with animals such as bison, wild boar, horse, and deer. So well conserved they are that their authenticity was at first highly doubted. These archaeological findings throughout Spain are among Europe's most impressive. The caves of Atapuerca and Altamira have both been declared World Heritage Sites by the United Nations Educational, Scientific, and Cultural Organization (UNESCO), whose goal is to encourage the identification, appreciation, protection, and preservation of outstanding natural and cultural monuments and heritage sites worldwide.

Gran Columna at Caves of Nerja

Evidence has been discovered of farming communities that existed in the southern part of the Iberian Peninsula during the 5th millennium BCE. These people are believed to have come from Africa (Libya), across the Straits of Gibraltar, and settled in Europe around 3000 BCE. Evidence also suggests that the Iberians may have come from the eastern shores of the Mediterranean Sea; or they may have been of North African Berber stock. The Greeks called them Iberians, as they first settled near the *Iberus* (Ebro) River and Valley.

The Basques are believed to be descendants of these early Iberians; they, too, derive their current name from one given to them by other people, later in history. The Romans called them *Vascones*, and from this the term "Basque" is derived. The Basques are an indigenous people of Western Europe as well as the oldest existing population to have occupied and inhabited the same particular region for over two millennia without interruption. Archaeological remains suggest that communities existed in the Basque region as long as 70,000 years ago. Many believe the Basques to be direct descendants of Cro-Magnon man.

As the Basques were surrounded by mountains, neither wars nor invasions have ever deterred these people, unlike other civilizations of ancient Europe. No link has ever been found between their language and that of any other; it is the only language in Western Europe that has not been classified as an Indo-European language. Archeological findings allow some scholars to theorize that the enigmatic Basque language, or *Euskera*, was spoken by the first Iberians, and there is a legend claiming it was also the language of Adam and Eve.

The Phoenicians, a thriving culture from the area that is today Lebanon and Syria, arrived around 1100 BCE and set up trading settlements in the southern towns of Málaga, Almuñecar and Cádiz. Their capital was established in Cádiz and it not only became a major harbor, but Europe's first urban community. The Phoenicians are believed to be the first people to have had commercial ties with Spain, via their trading posts along the coast of northern Africa. As a result of these foreign contacts, Spain was introduced to new mining techniques and commercial ideas as well as many wonderful commodities including musical instruments, the potter's wheel, domestic animals, vine cultivation, and the alphabet.

Between the 9th and 7th centuries BCE, Aryan Celts who migrated south and west from Europe across the Pyrenees merged with the Iberians and formed the Celt-Iberian tribe. These people, who dominated the northern regions, excelled in crafting metalwork, farming, and herding, and by the 6th century BCE their culture was well defined.

Spain was conquered by their Greek trading partners, who began settling along the eastern coast around the 8th century BCE. They founded colonies, including their main trading post at Ampurias, during the 6th century BCE, along the same stretch of the eastern Mediterranean shore that later flourished under the Romans. Many believe that it was the Greeks who introduced the vine and olive to Spain.

By 700 BCE, the semi-legendary Hispanic Kingdom of Tartessus prospered and spread throughout Andalusia and the eastern Mediterranean coast of the Levante to the north of Alicante. This mythical city is said to have been situated at the mouth of the Guadalquivir, near Cádiz. The Tartessians established important trading relations with the Phoenicians. However, by the 6th century BCE, the kingdom suddenly vanished from history, perhaps destroyed by the competing Carthaginians or due to the many floods and inundations that plagued the region circa 500 BCE. Some believe that Tartessus was in fact the biblical city of Tarshish, mentioned in the Old Testament.

Between the 6th and 4th century BCE the Carthaginians, descendants of the Phoenicians, migrated from the North African city of Carthage in present-day Tunisia. These explorers founded Cartagena as their capital on the southeastern coast of Spain around 230 BCE. Like the Greek and Phoenician settlers before them, the Carthaginians were attracted to Spain's mineral wealth. Due to its ideal location, Cartagena not only became one of the major coastal trading settlements in the region but one of the richest cities in the world.

The Carthaginians were permanently overthrown in Spain by the Romans during the Second Punic War (218-201 BCE). Their victory marked the beginning of Roman dominance over Spain, as the country was later divided into Roman provinces. The town and military outpost of *Itálica* was founded in the same year by General Scipio. Located about 7 miles north of Hispalis (Seville), Itálica was the birthplace of Roman emperors Trajan and Hadrian during the first century AD. Another important Roman figure was the statesman, philosopher, poet, and writer Seneca (c. 4 BCE-AD 65), whose birthplace was Córdoba, the capital of *Baética* (or southern Spain), as designated by Emperor Augustus.

Itálica, known today as Santiponce, is home to one of the most important and impressive Roman ruins in the peninsula, the imposing remains of a massive amphitheater said to have seated 40,000 spectators. By 19 BCE, the southern region known as *Hispania Baética* was declared a Roman province. Once the wealthiest province of the Roman Empire, Baética encompassed less territory than Andalusia does today. Its principal cities were Gades (Cádiz), Hispalis (Seville), and Córduba (Córdoba).

The transition was not effortless; it took the Romans two centuries to complete their mission of fully incorporating the newly conquered land into their empire. It was the Romans who laid the foundation for Spain's religion, government structure, laws, administration, and language that are still in effect today. During this time the production and trade of wine, wax, wheat, honey, pepper, and olive oil grew into a flourishing commerce. In turn, the new conquerors benefited from Spain's wealth in the form of iron, lead, tin, copper, silver, and gold mines, as well as gaining Spanish soldiers to fight for their Roman Empire.

At most, the population of Roman Spain at its peak is estimated at 6,000,000. Vast improvements were made by the industrious Romans in the construction of a road system that was originally built for military purposes. It has been estimated that over 17,500 miles of roadway were constructed throughout the peninsula. Other extensive building projects were undertaken, such as the construction of large cities, amphitheaters, temples, bridges, salting pits, sewage systems, and aqueducts. An outstanding example is the magnificent 128-arched aqueduct in Segovia which, after nearly two millennia, is still remarkably well conserved and stands in the center of the town. It is considered one of the best preserved examples of Roman architecture in the world.

Roman Aqueduct in Segovia

However, during the early part of the 5th century AD, the decline of the Roman Empire opened the door to invasions of Germanic tribes including the Alans, Vandals, and Sueves, who crossed the Pyrenees into Spain in 409. The Vandals marched deep into Spain and eventually succeeded in driving the Romans out, remaining in power until 428. These warriors renamed the land *Vandalusia;* they are said to have burned homes, raped women, slaughtered inhabitants, and destroyed the cities and crops wherever they went. Hence the origins of the term "vandalism."

The Romans called for help and to their aid came the slightly more civilized Visigoths, in 414, who ultimately succeeded in defeating the Vandals. For most of the 5th century, various battles between the Vandals and Visigoths took place. The Visigoths became the major political authority in Spain and by the end of the 5th century, they came into full power. These people were greatly influenced by the Romans and embraced Catholicism as their official state religion in 589.

The Visigoths were few in number, estimated at 300,000, while the rest of the population was almost 4 to 5 million at this time. Their capital was established in the city of Tolosa (Toulouse) in 419; they lost their kingdom in what is now southern France around the year 507. The Visigoths eventually rebuilt their kingdom and re-established a capital city at Toledo in central Spain. They ruled from here for the next two and a half centuries. The Visigoths left few traces of their stay and most of their churches have been rebuilt by other cultures that followed and converted them to their own places of worship.

The quality of life eventually declined under the chaotic Visigoth rule and they were no match for the next conquerors, who came during the early part of the 8th century. These people came to be known as the Moors in Spain but were in actuality mostly Berbers from North Africa who had converted to Islam and, in smaller numbers, Muslim Arabs who had migrated from the Middle East. The Visigoths were easily defeated by the Moors in 711 (the year 92, according to the Islamic calendar) and a period of nearly eight centuries of Muslim rule in Spain was established as a result.

Throughout the land, the Moors built stunning palaces and fortresses with magnificent gardens as well as mosques, markets, bath houses, and universities. They not only brought with them their religion but many aspects of their vibrant culture that undoubtedly influenced local customs still in effect today. Their long and powerful presence infiltrated and formed many aspects of Andalusí culture such as the arts, architecture, literature, cuisine, sciences, poetry, dance, and music. Many inhabitants left their cultural imprints in Spain; however, it was the Moors who contributed the most by transforming southern Spain into the most prosperous and advanced region of its time, shaping it into what it is today.

2. The Moors

In the year 710, a Berber officer named Tarif ibn Malik and his army of 400 men and 100 horses in four vessels crossed the Straits of Gibraltar from North Africa and disembarked at the southernmost tip of mainland Europe. His name would be immortalized at the spot where he landed, named *Tarifa* in his honor. Having met with little opposition from the Visigoths, Tarif eventually returned home with many riches; and the seed that grew into nearly eight centuries of Muslim rule in Spain was planted.

The following year armies comprised of 5,000 men, mostly Berbers with Arab and Syrian soldiers, were again sent under the command of Governor Musa ibn Nusayr across the Straits. Other sources have this number as high as 7,000 to 12,000 soldiers; that can best be explained as a result of additional men being sent to conquer and populate the land shortly afterwards. This expedition was led by Berber general and army leader named Tariq ibn-Ziyad, who disembarked at another spot, which likewise was named after him: Gibraltar, a corruption of *Gebel al-Tariq* or "Tariq's Mountain."

One account has it that the Muslim invasion of Spain began by way of an invitation to the Arab troops of North Africa to help the Byzantine governor of Ceuta, Count Julian, in dethroning the Visigoth king. According to ancient chronicles and ballads, Roderic or Rodrigo, the last king of the Spanish Visigoths, who began his rule from Toledo in 709, was a brute who had "his way" with a beautiful girl named Florinda, whom he fell in love with and kidnapped while she was bathing in the Rio Tajo. Florinda (also known as *Cava*) happened to be the youngest daughter of his friend Count Julian, who, upon hearing the news, became enraged and sought revenge against the Visigoths by allying with the Moors and sending forth the Moorish king Musa to invade Spain. This violent incident is, at least according to legend, the *casus belli* that led to the Islamic conquest of Spain. Of course, when a resource-rich region is the prize, would-be conquers are likely to come up with some justification for their campaigns.

By the time the Romans arrived in Spain, many Jewish immigrants had already settled throughout the land. They were treated quite harshly. Under the Visigoths, all Jews were declared slaves and their religion was prohibited. Further bans involved the construction of new synagogues and the forming of mixed marriages. During the 7th century, the Visigoths imposed upon the Jews a policy of forced conversion. Thus another theory regarding the onset of the Moorish invasion of Spain is that the Jewish population pleaded to the Arabs and Berbers for help.

By the 8th century, no other options were available to the Jews except converting to Christianity or risking expulsion from the peninsula. Thus the Jews did ally themselves with the Moors and they were instrumental in contributing to the decline of Visigoth rule in Spain. The Moors were welcomed by the oppressed and large Jewish community, who were then freed from slavery and permitted to form their own communities, as long as acknowledgement and respect was give to their Muslim rulers.

Tariq and his men easily conquered the declining Visigoth kingdom at the Battle of Guadalete in the summer of 711. Roderic died in battle on July 19 and Spain no longer had a leader. Tariq's mission now was to expand the Muslim empire by seizing control of the entire Iberian Peninsula and making it a division of the Umayyad Empire. In 712, Musa ibn Nusayr crossed the Straits of Gibraltar once again, this time with an army of 18,000 soldiers to share in the new-found wealth and assist in the expansion of the Muslim territory.

The immigrants who settled in al-Andalus were predominantly Berbers from North Africa. The capital was established in Seville (as English-speakers call Sevilla) in the year 713, but three years later when al-Andalus became a province of the Umayyad Empire, governed from Damascus, the capital was shifted to Córdoba.

However, Islamization did not proceed evenly throughout the entire peninsula, as the focus was mainly placed upon its southern region. The Moors basically occupied the major strongholds in the south that were former Roman colonies and important centers of civilization such as Córdoba, Seville, Granada and, in central Spain, Toledo. Within seven years, they conquered most of the country except a few small parts in the north and the Basque region in the Pyrenees. Toledo, once the capital of the Visigoth Kingdom, had a population of about 5,000 when it was overthrown by the Moors. When the Visigoths were defeated, a number of refugees left for the northern mountainous region and formed the Kingdom of Asturias.

Asturias was one of the few areas of the peninsula that the Moors were unable to fully conquer for long. Their hero was a nobleman of Visigoth descent named Pelayo, who had fought and managed to escape capture at the Battle of Guadalete. As Roderick's successor, Pelayo was determined to rebel against the Moors by creating his own Christian kingdom. Around 722, a century after the birth of Islam, Pelayo fought against Uthman ibn Naissa (better known as *Munuza*), the Moorish governor of Asturias and northern Spain. Pelayo defeated the Moorish army and Munuza lost his life in battle. Pelayo was elected King of Asturias and the town became the first established Christian nation of Spain since the Islamic conquest of 711. This event is known as the historically significant Battle of Covadonga that halted Arab expansion in this area while securing Asturias as a Christian stronghold. It represents the first Christian victory of the Reconquest that was to be fully finalized seven centuries later.

Nearly three-quarters of the country was under Muslim rule during the first three centuries after their arrival, with an estimated population of 250,000 Berbers and 50,000 Arabs. However, the Moors were not preoccupied with conquering the cold, northern parts of Spain. These under-developed mountainous areas were difficult to reach and were fiercely protected by their inhabitants.

Within the Iberian Peninsula, the Moors also conquered Portugal and incorporated it into their kingdom. The Portuguese Reconquest was completed towards the end of the 13th century when King Alfonso III drove the Moors out of the southernmost province of Algarve, ending nearly six centuries of Arab rule. The Christian capital was established in Lisbon and has remained there ever since. Traces of Moorish presence remain highly visible throughout Portugal, particularly in architecture, place names, and the old Moorish quarters such as the *Alfama*. Among the highlights is the 8th-century Moorish fortress named *Castelo of Jorge*, (Castle of Saint George), a former Visigoth fortification that overlooks Lisbon.

During the early part of the Muslim conquest of the Iberian Peninsula, their rulership also extended across the Pyrenees into southern France, as had that of the kingdom of the Visigoths. Expeditions to conquer Gaul (France) during the 8th century, headed under the command of governor *Abd al-Rahman al-Ghafiqi*, had some success. These expeditions began in 719 and within a decade, the Moors occupied such French southern cities as *Avignon, Carcasson*, as well as *Arbuna* (Narbonne). A year later, Arbuna became the Moorish capital of the former Visigoth province the Romans had previously named *Septimania*, or southern France.

Basilica Saint-Denis, Saint-Denis, France

For a short while it seemed that France could also become part of the Muslim Empire. However, in October of 732, the Moorish army was decisively defeated by a ruler who came to be known as Charles Martel (Charles the Hammer) as a result of his "striking" victory. At the *Battle of Tours*, also known as the *Battle of Poitiers*, governor Abd al-Rahman lost his life and, to the sheer astonishment of the French, the Moorish soldiers did not continue their mission but quietly retreated overnight. Charles Martel died in 741 and lies buried at the Saint-Denis Basilica in a northern industrial suburb of

Paris, along with such royalty as Louis XVI and Marie Antoinette as well as Henry II and Catherine de' Medici. This magnificent Gothic structure built over Gallo-Roman cemetery is considered a masterpiece and has been the final resting place of French royalty since the 7th century.

It was not until 759 that Arbuna was recaptured by the French, taken by a son of Charles Martel named Pepin the Short, effectively terminating the possibility of Muslim rule in France. However, futile Muslim expeditions and raids into France did continue into the 11th century.

Although the Moors were ultimately unsuccessful in conquering France, one wonders if it really was a victory for the French at that particular time in history. While Córdoba was enjoying its Golden Age during the 10th century, other cities in Europe remained in the Dark Ages. Córdoba, with a population of over half a million, had running water and streets that were paved and lighted seven centuries before London and Paris.

Statue of Abd al-Rahman I in Almuñecar, Granada

FOUNDER OF AL-ANDALUS

Abd al-Rahman ibn Mu'awiyah al Dakhil (Abderahman, to the Spaniards) was a young prince born into the Umayyad Dynasty of Damascus. He was not only half Berber and half Syrian, but also a blood relation of Tariq ibn-Ziyad. In 750 the Umayyad Dynasty was overthrown by the rivaling *Abbasids* from Baghdad who claimed to be descendants from Muhammad's uncle *Abbas*. Internal struggles between these two dynasties led to the massacre of the entire Umayyad family at a banquet that the Abbasids set up with deadly ulterior motives. The only survivor was the 20-year-old Abd al-Rahman, who five years later, after traveling through the desert of North Africa as a fugitive, decided to run away to southern Spain.

In the summer of 755, the prince arrived at what is now a charming fishing village off the Tropical Coast town of Almuñécar in Granada. Here his striking image is cast in a large bronze statue situated below a large rock leading out to the sea known as *El Peñon del Santo*.

Commemorating this event, the inscription reads: "El 15 de agosto de 755 DC, Abderrahman I 'El Emigrante' procedente de Damasco por la Playa de Almuñécar, siendo el creador del floreciente Estado de al-Andalus." ("On the 15th of August in AD 755, Abderrahman I, 'The Emigrant,' entered Spain from Damascus through the beach of Almuñécar, thus becoming the creator of the flourishing State of al-Andalus.")

In the year 756, Abd al-Rahman founded a semi-independent Emirate in Córdoba and became the first Emir whose dynasty would rule here for nearly three centuries more. Internal strife between the Arabs and Berbers decreased during his rule and Córdoba became the center of the western Emirate, replacing Damascus as the residence of their dynasty. Not only was this city the most advanced center of learning in Europe, but it was also the new capital of the Islamic world.

Abd al-Rahman died in 788 and was succeeded by his son Hisham I (r. 788-796) who in turn was succeeded by his son al-Hakam I (r. 796-822), who was the father of Abd al-Rahman II.

ABD AL RAHMAN II AND III

Abd al-Rahman II came into power in 822 and is credited with instituting military reform, improving neighboring relations with other provinces, and building mosques throughout al-Andalus as well as expanding the great Mosque in Córdoba. Abd al-Rahman II also established a monopoly over the minting of coins during his thirty-year reign. He was responsible for introducing southern Spain to literature, as he sent forth scholars to Persia to bring back and translate works on the subjects of science, philosophy, astronomy, medicine, theology, and music.

However, in January of 929, a completely independent Caliphate from Baghdad was formed in Córdoba by Abd al-Rahman III. A man of short stature born in Córdoba with fair complexion and blue eyes, who reportedly died his red hair black in order to appear Moorish, was not only the first Caliph in Spain but is regarded as the greatest leader of the Umayyad Dynasty. Under his rule, Córdoba flourished culturally, socially, intellectually, and politically, rivaling that of any other capital in the world of its time.

Abd al-Rahman III completely severed Spain's ties with Baghdad and proclaimed himself the first Caliph. He successfully set out to prove to the world that his court in Córdoba equaled or was even greater than theirs. Under his rule, al-Andalus flourished as a major center of Muslim power, experienced economic prosperity, and benefited from great intellectual, scientific, agricultural, and cultural advancement. He is also responsible for the construction of the once palatial city of *Medina Azahara* in Córdoba.

Medina Azahara in Córdoba

Abd al-Rahman III had a thirst for knowledge and imported many books from Baghdad. Eventually philosophers, scholars, historians, musicians and the like began to arrive and settle in al-Andalus. As a result, many libraries, research institutes and places of learning arose that distinguished southern Spain from the rest of the world as it continued to thrive as a center of advanced studies in such fields as medicine, science, literature, and philosophy.

After the death of Abd al-Rahman III in 961, Al-Andalus continued to flourish under the command of al-Hakam II or *Alhakén II* and Muslim general *Ibn Abi Amir*, better known by the title he claimed for himself in 981, *Al-Mansur*, meaning "The Victorious." *Almanzor*, as he is known to the Spaniards, was born in Algecíras, Cádiz and arrived in Córdoba as a student of law and literature. He organized and successfully accomplished numerous military campaigns against the Christian states of Spain and has been credited with no less than 50 such victories. It is no wonder that al-Mansur quickly rose and became the equivalent in al-Andalus of the Grand Vizier in the Muslim East. Almanzor ordered the construction of another palatial city in Córdoba, known as *Medina Zahira*.

By the end of the 11th century, nearly all the lower half of the Iberian Peninsula was under Moorish rule. During the 12th and 13th centuries, Muslims, Jews, and Christians continued to live peacefully together under Islamic rule. While such tolerance was unheard of in the rest of Europe, in al-Andalus, Christians and Jews living under Arabic rule did so in relative harmony. Mixed marriages were also permitted at this time. The Moors showed great tolerance towards those with Visigoth and Hispano-Roman ancestors and allowed the Jews and Christians to maintain their religious beliefs and practices, as long as their Muslim rulers were respected and accepted. The Moors in turn respected or at least tolerated the Jews and Christians, who acknowledged their second-class citizen roles and paid their taxes.

This small population of non-Muslim citizens were known as *Dhimmīs*, or "The Protected Ones." The Dhimmis were subjected to various restrictions and paid extra census taxes known as *Jizyah*. They were treated better than other religious minorities that lived throughout Europe during this time. However, the Dhimmis were not allowed to build new synagogues or churches and were instructed to follow their own religion privately, indoors. Nothing was permitted that would go against Islam. Severe punishment awaited the Dhimmi who challenged the Islamic faith. The Dhimmis were prohibited from giving orders to Muslims and therefore were banned from being employers or holding public office. However, this rule was not always observed as many were, indeed, employed by Caliphs in responsible positions as they proved themselves to be quite dependable and hardworking.

Life among the three faiths in al-Andalus was fairly peaceful; however, there were several periods of great strife. Let us not forget that many Jews and Christians were forced into slavery, deported, or even massacred. Numerous Christians perished in Toledo after revolting against the Moors in 713. Seventy-two people were crucified in Córdoba during the year 805 for devising a conspiracy plan against the Emir.

During the middle of the 9th century, Muslims responded to a small Christian movement of extremists that publicly confronted Islam and openly maligned the prophet Muhammad. This group of 48 individuals, made up of mostly Christian monks and priests, became known as the *Martyrs of Córdoba*. Without provocation from the Arabs, they set out to dissuade Christian youths from assimilating to the Arabic culture and language. Their mission failed and the Martyrs of Córdoba were executed by Islamic authorities.

As well, thousands of Spanish Jews died in Córdoba and Granada during the 11th century, in Toledo during the 12th century, and in Seville during the 14th century. Jews and Christians also suffered under the hands of the *Almoravides* and *Almohad* Berber tribes, who inflicted great destruction upon their cultures between the 11th and 13th centuries. More attacks upon Christians ensued in Toledo in 1467.

THE TAIFA RULERS

After the greatness of the Golden Age, Muslim power began to wane towards the middle of the 11th century. It marked the beginning of the end of Islamic rule in Spain. Internal struggles among the small kingdoms resulted in a period of decline that eventually led to the total collapse and overthrow of the Caliphate in Córdoba. The triggering event was the death of the last Umayyad Caliph *Hisham III al-Mu'tadd* in the year 1031. Upon his demise, al-Andalus, formerly unified under Muslim rule, became divided into many small kingdoms or politically weak independent states known as *Taifas*.

These states were ruled by local families of Arabic aristocracy and by Berber military groups. The largest of the Taifas were Córdoba, Granada, Seville, and Málaga. Their rule extended as far as Toledo in central Spain, Valencia in the east, Zaragoza in the northeast, and Badajoz in the west.

It was far from peaceful among the Taifa kings. It was a time of anarchy and confusion and the seams began to tear, facilitating the triumph of Christianity over Islam that was rapidly approaching.

In desperation, the Taifa kings requested help in 1086 from the Almoravides in fighting against the Christian kings of Castile and León. The Almoravides were not only fervently religious, but were quite proficient in military tactics as well. The Christians were defeated and the Almoravides returned to Spain in 1090 to reconquer the land for themselves. This was accomplished within a year and al-Andalus was once again re-united, but only as a province administered by governors sent forth by the Almoravid Emir of Marrakesh.

In 1090, Castilian hero and Christian conqueror *Rodrigo Díaz de Vivar*, better known as *El Cid*, started a campaign against the Almoravides who were advancing into eastern Spain. El Cid actually fought on both Muslim and Christian sides throughout his military career. Although his loyalties wavered, he ultimately captured the region of Valencia from the Moors four years later and presented it to King Alfonso. As a reward, El Cid was made the ruler of Valencia in 1094, where he died peacefully five years later. It is generally believed that his triumphs prevented the Islamic invasion of Western Europe during the 11th century by facilitating the onset of the Reconquest.

The epic poem that immortalized El Cid's conquests as a Christian hero was written several hundred years after his death. Titled *Poema (or Cantar) de Mio Cid*, ("Poem" or "Song of My Cid"), it was anonymously written during the 12th century. It stands as the earliest surviving sample of Castilian epic poetry preserved in its entirety, as well as the first great work of Spanish literature. Two excerpts from the verses read:

> Mio Çid Ruy Diaz por las puertas entrava,
> En mano trae desnuda el espada,
> Quinze moros matava de los que alcançava.

> My lord Rodrigo Díaz, through the gates he would enter,
> A sword naked in his hand, he slew 15 Moors before him.

> Allí vierais tantas lanzas subir y bajar,
> Tanta adarga horadar y pasar,
> Tanta loriga romper y rajar,
> Tantos pendones blancos rojos de sangre quedar,

Tantos buenos caballos sin sus dueños andar.
Oyerais a unos, «¡Mahoma!»; a otros, «¡Santiago!» gritar.
Yacían por el campo en poco lugar mil y trescientos moros muertos,
  ya.

There you will see so many spears rising and falling,
So many leather shields piercing and soaring.
So much armor breaking and tearing,
So many white banners stained red with blood.
So many fine horses without their masters,
While the Moors cry "Muhammad" and Christians "Santiago,"
In the fields already lie one thousand three hundred slain Moors.

Almoravid rule ended when the dynasty was overthrown in 1147 by the Almohads, an even more fanatical Berber sect from the Atlas Mountains of today's Morocco. However, in 1212 the Almohads were defeated in turn by Christian armies at the battle of *Las Navas de Tolosa* under the leadership of Alfonso VIII of Castile. In 1224, another Berber dynasty from Morocco known as *Banu Marins* (Children of Marins) or *Marinids* attempted to invade the land. Although they were not successful in Spain, they defeated the Almohads in Morocco 45 years later.

The Last Muslim Dynasty

In 1232, *Muhammad ibn Yusuf ibn Nasr* founded the last Muslim dynasty in Spain known as the *Nasrids*. Born in Jaén to the *Banu Nasr* in 1195, he became known as *Al-Hamar*, meaning "The Red," as this was the color of his beard and hair. It is said that his fortune was told at birth by astrologers who cast his horoscope and predicted a victorious life. According to local legend, the moment Al-Hamar took his first breath on earth an angel mounted on a magnificent white horse appeared in the starry sky waving a luminous flag with the inscription, *"Wa la ghalib illa Allah,"* meaning, "There is no conqueror but Allah." Al-Hamar not only founded the last Muslim dynasty in Spain, but he began the construction of the majestic Alhambra six years later; this famous phrase is immortalized throughout the complex.

By 1240, Granada extended along the coast from Murcia (north of Almería) to Tarifa, encompassing part of the actual provinces of Málaga, Cádiz, Seville, Córdoba, Jaén, Almería, and Granada itself. In order to maintain Granada, Al-Hamar helped the king of Castile conquer Seville in 1248 by supplying troops to the Christian side. When the Muslim king returned to Granada, he was hailed as a conqueror; to this he quickly objected and spoke the celebrated phrase, *Wa la ghalib illa Allah*, which became the motto of the Nasrid Dynasty. (Nevertheless, he did assume the title of *al-Ghalib*, or "the Conqueror.") Al-Hamar died in 1273 and his rich and successful life had indeed fulfilled the astrologers' predictions.

Granada managed to survive until the end of the 15th century by paying heavy tribute to the Catholic kings. Indeed, it prospered; refugees from other cities that had fallen to the Christians began to settle here and as a result Granada expanded and flourished. One can say that its "golden age" took place during the 13th and 14th centuries when many advancements were made in commerce, culture, and art.

Like the Taifas of the 11th century, the other cities of al-Andalus began to crumble. Córdoba fell to the Christians in 1236, Jaén in 1246, and Seville in 1248. By 1251, al-Andalus was part of the Christian Empire, all except the Kingdom of Granada — that included Almería as of 1237 and Málaga as of 1239. The kingdom survived with a population estimated at 300,000 for over two centuries more.

In 1469 *Fernando* of the Kingdom of Aragón married *Isabella* of the Kingdom of Castile, and together they ruled as the King and Queen of Spain. The marriage cemented the union of Christian Spain as León, Galicia, Asturias, and Catalonia were united under their new kingdom. The Reconquest that began during the 11th century was, after four centuries, set into full motion as all Muslims and Jews were ordered to convert to Christianity or be expelled from the land. *Los Reyes Católicos*, or the "Catholic Monarchs," a title bestowed upon them by Pope Alexander VI in 1494 for their victory over Granada, were determined to enforce Christianity in Spain even at the cost of many deaths.

The Spanish Inquisition began in 1480 and was directed at those who did not accept Catholicism. Those who failed to convert or flee were persecuted, tortured, and executed after being publicly condemned under the religious act or trial known as the *Auto de Fe* or "Act of Faith." The first such act took place in Seville on February 6th, 1481. As a result, six accused men and women were condemned to death and burned at the stake at the hands of Fernando and Isabella. The number of victims estimated during its history varies significantly, ranging from nearly 4,000 to over 30,000, making it an atrocity verging on cultural genocide. It is believed that during the first 12 years of the Spanish Inquisition, over 13,000 "heretics" were tried and the number to have perished at the stake throughout its lengthy history is likely in the hundreds. The Catholic Church states that only 1% of the 125,000 people tried as suspected heretics were actually executed in Spain. Renowned British novelist and traveler George Borrow (1803-1811) states that the Jews were persecuted and expelled from Spain on the basis of their penchant for higher learning and intellect as well as for their aptitude for accumulating great riches and wealth. He further proposes that Moriscos were also expelled from the country because of their superior talents in trade, manufacturing, and engineering that inspired envy among Christian Spaniards.

Abu abd-Allah, also known as *Muhammad XII* and *Boabdil el Chico* to the Spaniards, was the last Muslim ruler of the Nasrid Dynasty. Boabdil inherited the throne from his father and came into power in 1482. A decade later, Los Reyes Católicos finally drove the Moors and Jews out of Granada, the last remaining Muslim stronghold of the Iberian Peninsula. On January 2, 1492, Boabdil was forced to surrender the keys to Granada and relinquish the land to the Catholic Kings, leaving his beloved city behind. It is said that he took one last look over his shoulder at the magnificent Alhambra as nearly 800 years of Islamic rule in al-Andalus came to a crushing end. The mournful point where he stood one final moment contemplating his loss is known as *El Ultimo Suspiro del Moro*, or "The Last Sigh of the Moor," and is situated on the road from Granada to Motril. Legend has it that Boabdil's mother *Aixa* harshly asked her son, "Why do you weep like a woman for the loss of what you could not defend like a man?" Boabdil is believed to have been compensated 30, 000 dinars and retreated to the Alpujarra Mountains south of Granada, to later migrate to Morocco. Some say he died there a broken man in 1527, betrayed by his wife, ridiculed by his mother, and defeated by the Catholic Kings. Others believe that he was killed in Morocco while fighting in battle.

During the Reconquest, a massive influx of Muslims and Jews fleeing Spain arrived in Morocco. However a number did choose to stay and remain faithful to Islam under Christian rule; they were known as *Mudéjares*. At first, the Mudéjares were permitted to practice their own religion and customs and speak their own language, and were subject to their own Islamic laws, but by 1502 the Mudéjares also had to convert to Christianity or leave Spain.

It was in this year that King Fernando and Queen Isabella declared all inhabitants of Spain to be Roman Catholics.

The Mudéjares who remained after the Reconquest and underwent forced baptism became known as *Moriscos*, or "Moor-like." In 1566, Felipe II renewed the laws set under the Edict of 1526 that forbade their colorful silk garments, their festivities and public baths, as well as the traditional use of henna by the women. Maintaining Moorish names was also against the law, so that their ancestry would eventually be forgotten. The Moriscos were banned from owning African slaves that came from The Gambia, Senegal, and Guinea, as well as prohibited from celebrating any family event such as a birth, wedding, and the mourning a family death.

The use of their language at all, on any occasion, whether in speaking or writing, was also forbidden and was punishable as a crime under this royal decree. They were given three years to learn the language of Christian Spain and so the Moriscos created a new language of their own, derived from the local Romance dialect (Vulgar Latin) but written in Arabic script. This colloquial Andalusian language was called *al-Ajamiyah*, or *Aljamía*, meaning "The Foreign," and pronounced *Aljamiado* in Castilian. It is essentially Mozárabic or Medieval Spanish written in Arabic script.

Aljamía was used for everyday purposes and was the language that Moriscos used to translate and therefore retain all their Muslim prayers and proverbs. The earliest reference of this language is in an anonymous botanical treaty found dated from the 9th century.

The Moriscos were under constant close surveillance and were forced to pay heavy taxes. Even the use of the word "Morisco" became punishable. Victims were banned from seeking employment as shoemakers, silversmiths, pottery makers, bakers, jewelers, cauldron makers, and blacksmithing. The Moriscos were demoted to work in manual labor such as farming, agriculture, and pasturing.

This was the catalyst for the revolt of the Granada Moriscos that began two years later, in 1568, known as the *Second Rebellion of Alpujarra*. This uprising resulted in large massacres and forced mass relocation of over 80,000 Moriscos from Granada in 1571 to other regions of the Peninsula, particularly in Castile, so that they could be integrated with others and eventually fade away. However, many remained secret Muslims, living one life privately, indoors, separate from the one they lived outdoors, in public. Even those who did accept Catholicism were nevertheless constantly suspected of secretly continuing their own religious practices, and eventually the Moriscos or Christian Moors were no longer tolerated nor accepted. To a large extent they were persecuted and expelled on the basis of their ethnicity rather than their religion, as they had publicly accepted and converted to Christianity as the law demanded.

It has been estimated that about half a million Moriscos were expelled from Spain between 1609 and 1611. Many Moriscos from Granada fled to the mountains of the Alpujarras, becoming bandits or outlaws, called *monfíes* by the Christians. The monfíes attacked the townspeople sporadically, becoming a cause of concern to the Christians as tensions increased between the two.

During the beginning of the 17th century an estimated 7500 Moriscos lived in Seville, more than any other city in the country. Within five years after King Felipe III ordered the expulsion of all Moriscos, Jews, and Gypsies, an estimated 300,000 Moriscos left Spain, mostly fleeing to Morocco, Algeria, and Tunisia. What came next were years of social chaos, political instability, cultural demise, and economical collapse resulting in the spiraling downfall of Spain. Although the end of al-Andalus was inevitable at this point, Andalusí culture managed to survive in small areas after the Reconquest for over a century and, quite fortunately, exerted an indisputable influence on the culture of Andalusia that is highly appreciated today.

Let us take a look at what life was like centuries ago in the land the Moors once ruled and named al-Andalus.

3. Al-Andalus

In al-Andalus, the Moors lived in their own neighborhoods or *Morerías*, and by the middle of the 14th century there were over a thousand throughout the land. The Jewish population lived in their own quarters called *Juderías* with their synagogues. These were small suburbs housing about 400 families each and were basically designed in the same format as the Morerías. Typical construction consisted of a group of houses around an interior patio surrounded by a wall with a gate. The most important Juderías were located in Seville, Córdoba, Jeréz, and, in the north, Tudela.

The Medina

The Moorish city or urban center of al-Andalus was known as the *Medina* and was comprised of narrow and winding streets protected by means of two gates that were closed at night. During the 10th century, the Medina of the Caliphate capital of Córdoba was surrounded and protected by a stone wall with seven doors of iron. The medinas were situated where the old Roman and Visigoth cities once stood. The plan differed from that of their predecessors that had been constructed in a rectangular shape. Roman cities were also enclosed by walls but had two main streets crossing each other, one running from north to south and the other from east to west. Leading away from some of the main streets that connected to the center of the Medina and extended to the suburbs were secondary streets that were irregular, winding, and quite narrow. From these sprang other lanes or alleys that terminated in dead ends or were closed by doors that provided access to homes.

The medina was the heart of the city where the mosque, markets, baths, administrative centers, and merchant inns were situated. This was the only part of the city dotted with squares, plazas, and streets wide enough to allow social and public commercial activities to take place. The inner city was divided in two zones, the commercial and the residential. Outside the city limits were the cemeteries or *maqbaras*. It has been estimated that during the 11th and 12th centuries, there were no fewer than 13 cemeteries in Córdoba.

The growing population of the medina gave way to *arrabales* or *harat* that were smaller suburbs constructed outside the perimeters of the enclosed Medina. Córdoba alone had over 20 such enclaves, each with its own smaller mosque, public baths, and markets or *Zocos*.

The Zoco

Social and commercial activities were limited to the market and mosque area within the town limits where narrow streets and squares allowed for such transactions. The great bazaar or *Suq al-Kebir* was situated on the main streets of the medina by the mosque. This permanent market was comprised of several streets with shops aligned around an open square where people congregated, conducted business, and offered their services. Varied merchandise was sold at stands by merchants who specialized in a specific craft or trade.

The bazaars were monitored by the *zabazoque*, later known as the *almotacén*, who functioned as an overseer and officer for the market. This inspector, whose duties were many, assigned assistants to help with such tasks as setting prices to avoid a monopoly, performing quality and health control, inspecting weights and measures, and imposing penalties when laws were broken. During the evening, this area was not only closed by locking gates at each entrance for protection against theft and vandalism, but was also patrolled by night guards.

The Zoco was also a place for socializing and recreation, where charmers and acrobats often performed for the crowds. During the 9th century, people gathered around and listened to the *rawi* who narrated or recited epic legends and love stories with great gesticulation in prose and in verse. Often, they were accompanied by musicians, similar to those found today in the Zocos of Marrakech and other Moroccan cities. These entertainers continued to be very much in demand within the Christian courts after the Reconquest.

In the main market you would find lawyers, doctors, pharmacists, booksellers, tailors, blacksmiths, silversmiths, goldsmiths, bricklayers, carpenters, painters, barbers, millers, shoemakers, dyers, tanners, potters, artisans, millers, butchers, and fishermen. Their shops and offices occupied the smaller premises situated nearby or at times were found by the mosque or warehouse where expensive merchandise was kept. Often, merchants such as weavers and livestock merchants set up shop in the *arrabales* or smaller neighborhoods outside the city due to the need for larger space — or because of the unhealthy smells or fumes, such as those emitted by tanners and oil merchants.

Alcaizería in Granada

In the food market, a myriad of aromatic herbs and spices such as mint, nutmeg, cumin, black pepper, caraway, coriander, parsley, and saffron — introduced to al-Andalus by the Moors — were always in abundance. Many varieties of vegetables, citrus fruits, meats, fish, and game were also sold.

14th Century Corral de Carbon in Granada

At the entrance to the Zoco was a smaller section that sold finer merchandise, known as the *Alcaicería*. The Alcaicería was a closed and covered market; there clothiers stored and sold luxury goods such as silk, wool, jewellery, and perfumes. The Alcaicería could also be situated on several streets or it might be formed by narrow alleys aligned with merchant shops. During the night these premises were also guarded by watchmen and closed off by gates. The reconstructed Alcaicería of Granada today is now a lively and enchanting area of small streets and alleys filled with Spanish and Moroccan souvenir and crafts shops where the Great Bazaar once stood. Nearby you will find the charming street known as *Zacatín*, by the Cathedral. This was the old clothes and silk market at the lower part of the street by the river bank that once existed where textiles and cloth were sold. Nowadays, the Alcaicería is a marketplace selling high quality (expensive) souvenirs such as embossed leather goods, ceramics, embroidery, crafts, brass, silver, as well as fine jewellery and more.

In al-Andalus, merchants and retailers from out of town who were tending to business within the market often stayed at nearby inns or *Alhóndigas*. Here they stored their goods and engaged in transactions including the buying and selling of goods as well as the arrangement and distribution of the merchandise to the shops within the Zoco. These inns were either privately owned or were run by the royal Court and accommodated merchants from other nearby cities as well as from North Africa and the Near East. The *alhóndigas* were comprised of three floors that opened up to a patio with a small fountain and a decorative cistern or pond in the center. The first storey housed the warehouse and stables and the other two floors were used as an inn where merchants lodged. Also in Granada you will find the last remaining perfectly preserved alhóndiga, known as *Corral de Carbon*, that is also the town's oldest building.

Financial transactions were executed with money minted in Córdoba. Coins were struck in different values and inscribed with Arabic calligraphy, such as gold *dinars* (from the Roman *denarius*), silver *dirhams* (from the Greek *drachma*), and copper *feluses* ("money" in Arabic), each minted according to the royal standard. The first Andalusí mint was established in Córdoba; it produced coins from gold imported across the Sahara. At this time this monetary exchange system reached its peak in production. Abd al-Rahman I introduced a silver coin based on the dirham and during the reign of Abd al-Rahman II, were produced with the inscription, "There is no god but god, he is unique, and Muhammad is his messenger." In 929, Abd al-Rahman III was the first to mint quarter dinars and gold dinars issued in his name — rather than acknowledging Allah or Muhammad, as had always been done in the past. During the 12th century, the Almohads introduced the minting of square dirhams and the custom of engraving a square within the round coin that became extremely popular and was duplicated by the Christians years later.

HOMES

Home was a refuge to the people of al-Andalus as life was mostly spent outdoors. On the outside, the houses were generally modest and rarely revealed the social status of its particular inhabitants. They did however all share the same important need for comfort, intimacy, and privacy. Better homes had plumbing, running water, and often had elaborate fountains not only for aesthetic purposes but to bring a sense of tranquility through the sound of trickling water.

The houses actually varied little from those of their Roman predecessors; a hallway led past a series of private open spaces to an interior patio in the center of the home. The concept of having an interior patio goes back to the days of the Roman Empire. Homes in al-Andalus were constructed in this manner, with the living room, kitchen, and bedroom opening up to the patio. The patio was paved with slabs of stone and often housed a ceramic cistern or fountain that was adorned with flowers and plants. This was the core of the home, and that is where most of family life took place. The patio provided light to the other rooms, as windows were small and few, and often were covered with shutters for privacy.

All homes had a *zaguán* or vestibule at the entrance, where guests were greeted. The largest rooms were rectangular with small alcoves found at each end. Matting or woven carpets of wool covered the tamped earth floors inside, and soft cushions of silk were found in every good household. The more affluent residences had decorated tiles covering their floors or rich carpets and tapestries for adornment. For warmth, a brazier holding burning coals was effectively used. The lavatory emptied out into a pit or through the sewage pipe or *alcantarilla* onto the streets.

In Andalusia the modest kitchen was found near the entrance of the home. Meals were cooked in a small cylindrical or truncated furnace excavated within the earth that operated on vegetable coal where different fried or boiled plates were prepared. Dishes made of stoneware were kept in large chests or cupboards and other household goods were kept in large chests. In wealthier homes, a pantry by the kitchen stored pitchers, wineskins, vats, and jars containing nutritional provisions for the year ahead.

The Andalusí diet consisted of meats, rice, vegetables, fruits, sweets, as well as many aromatic herbs and spices. Spices in particular were frequently used in the cooking of al-Andalus. Most of the spices sold at the Zoco were unknown to Spain before the arrival of the Moors. The recipes for most of the sweets consumed in the Iberian Peninsula today are actually of Arabic origin, made of such typical ingredients as almonds, nuts, sugar, and honey.

The most popular meat was lamb; which the poorer classes only tasted on special occasions. Varied fish was consumed in abundance by those who lived near the coast. Fish was highly prized by the Moors and was consumed in many different forms. It was often stuffed with spices and bread, fried in olive oil, prepared in a stew, or even pickled in vinegar and spices. It has been said that the idea of stuffing dishes in Spain is also of Arabic origin.

GARDENS

One of the many great contributions the Arabs gave to Andalusia was the innovative agricultural, hydraulic technology that produced great advances in botany, yielding magnificent gardens of flowers, plants, and trees. The Moors experimented with many exotic plant species and vastly improved the types that were already in existence. Among other floral species that were cultivated in al-Andalus were the rose, narcissus, iris, violet, wallflower, poppy, daisy, and jasmine.

The custom of these rich Islamic gardens (or *al-riat*) began in Córdoba and culminated in the magnificent gardens of the Alhambra and Generalife in Granada. Abd al Rahman I built a summer residence and country palace just outside the capital of Córdoba. These retreats, surrounded by pleasure gardens and cultivated land, were known as *almunias*, from the Arabic "al-Mounia." The Emir named this one *al-Rusafa*, in memory of the one he left behind in Damascus. Almunias not only served as summer retreats for recreation and relaxation but were also quite important in terms of agriculture as they were surrounded by extensive garden parks. Al-Rusafa was actually the first landscaped property of al-Andalus that became famous for its exotic plants and trees. Abd al-Rahman, who was passionate about botany, imported and transplanted all kinds of exotic plants and trees from his former home in Syria and other places to Córdoba. Among the many species that he introduced to al-Andalus was the palm tree.

CLOTHING

The typical clothing worn in Caliphal Córdoba, by peasants and noblemen alike, was a robe or tunic known in Castilian as a *saya* and in Arabic as *shaya*. The sleeved tunic had been the basic garment worn by Visigoths and Romans before. Oriental-style fashions were mainly reserved for members of the courts.

The wealthy wore woolen capes or cloaks as well as fur vests during colder months. Women wore long robes down to the ankles, with a scarf worn over the shoulders or above the head and down the shoulders, called *almalafa*. Another type of almalafa, similar to a cape or mantle, was worn by the wealthy. Women did not have to be veiled; in fact, it was uncommon in al-Andalus. However, they did often wrap their head in kerchiefs or scarves. It is from a few pieces of poetry that we know that women of all classes often dressed unveiled and that they sometimes wore veils that just covered the lower face.

Men wore loose-fitting pants under their robes that were gathered at the ankle. The poorer classes wore a similar, but shorter style, while the wealthier worn fine silk garments embroidered with gold threads produced in the textile workshops of Almería, Granada, Málaga, and Murcia.

During the 10ᵗʰ century a type a silk cloth with golden embroidery known as *almaizar* was introduced to al-Andalus. It came in various colors and was worn as a headband, veil or turban and also could be used to decoratively hold a hood in place. The turban never really caught on in al-Andalus; however, Berber soldiers did wear turbans during the Taifa period. By the end of Almohad rule, the turban was restricted to men of the law, particularly within the courts of the Nasrid Kingdom of Granada.

The Jewish population had to wear identifying clothing, such as a yellow turban or woolen cap, to distinguish them from the Muslims and Catholics. The Jews generally adopted the clothing style of the Moors that included the long robe with a belt. However, they were not permitted to don a belt in the color of green, that being the traditional color of Islam, nor were they allowed to wear such luxuries as silk fabrics or furs.

HAREMS

The harem or *harén* were the women, wives and concubines, that lived in a particularly affluent Arab household. The concept of the harem goes back to the ancient Babylonians, Persians, and Egyptians, and is generally associated with Muslim traditions as the Koran allows for multiple wives and concubines.

The harem could consist of a large room or it might occupy an entire wing of a residence where the women congregated and performed their domestic tasks. The secluded harem was constructed in such a manner that from the street, the interior was not visible to prying eyes. The windows or little balconies had wooden shutters known as *ajimeces* in order to allow the women to see and not be seen. Access was only permitted to male family members or very close male acquaintances. The women of the harem included all female relatives of the Caliph as well as his several wives and concubines. Heirs could be born to different mothers within the harem, and each male child was equally entitled to be in line for the throne.

Thousands of Christian women were recruited from Europe as slaves for the harems of the Caliphs of Spain. These women were especially popular as their lighter skin was rare and preferred. The women of al-Andalus actually enjoyed more freedom here than anywhere else in the Muslim world. Access to education provided women opportunities to reach high positions in a desired field or occupation. Many women from the harem were highly respected as they attained success in such areas as education, medicine, and music.

The favorite among the harem was usually the one who was most talented in singing or dancing. Abd al-Rahman III was so captivated by a concubine named *Zahra* that he built and named an entire magnificent city (*Madinat az-Zahra*) in her honor during the 10th century.

Ruins of Medina Azahara in Córdoba

THE HAMMAM

Another characteristic of traditional Islamic architecture in Spain was the abundance of the public baths or *hammam*, essential for Muslim religious and hygienic purposes. Their fondness for water and bath houses was abundantly introduced to al-Andalus and an estimated 700 baths were believed to have existed in Córdoba alone when it was the thriving center of Islamic Spain. The bath houses were usually situated at the entrance of the Medina where travellers could purify their body and souls before entering the city.

The bath houses served for religious purposes as the Muslim faith requires bathing before prayer several times a day. Hygiene is regarded as an expression of faith and devotion as cleanliness purifies both body and soul. The fact that hygiene was regarded as being conducive to physical and spiritual well-being is reflected in this saying that circulated in the bath houses of al-Andalus: "In Córdoba, a beggar would rather spend his last *dirham* on soap before spending it on bread." Washington Irving, in his *Tales of the Alhambra*, wrote about the significance of water to the Moors. "The Moors ... were indefatigable in their exertions to obtain that element in its crystal purity."

Like the smaller Roman bath houses, they were a daily meeting place for men (and women) of all walks of life to relax, congregate, and socialize, as well as for conducting political or business discussions and negotiations. Some hammams were modest and others most luxurious, with tiled walls embellished by elaborate columns, detailed arcs, marble fountains, intricate archways, and domed ceilings. The baths were characterized by skylights that allowed steam to escape and soft beams of light to enter. The lavatories were located on a lower level, with a separate entrance. Also on this level the firewood was stored and the boiler or *al-burma* was situated. The temperature was controlled by means of an underground air conductor that was heated by the boiler. The water came from aqueducts and waterwheels that were driven by donkeys.

The Arabic baths or *baños arabes* were divided into separate rooms (*bayt*) or chambers of varying temperatures, progressing from cold to hot. The first area was the vestibule, wardrobe, and resting room known as the *Bayt al-Musalaj*. This was a passage area of a long hall dotted with skylights in geometric shapes such as octagonal and hexagonal, or in the shape of stars, that served for both lighting and ventilation purposes. Known as *madawi*, these small apertures throughout the hammams also helped reduce the weight of the heavy ceilings.

Here the guest was greeted or enjoyed pleasantries with others, and often this area contained a drinking fountain, small patio, and lavatory. The first of the three main rooms was the cold room or *Bayt al-Barid*. On hot days this was where the guests left their clothing behind and donned a robe or towel and wooden slippers. The water was kept around 15°C, and often a massage was enjoyed before entering the warm room or *Bayt al-Wastani*. In this central and largest area, the water was kept around 35°C, where massages were also received. When the weather was colder, the clothing was removed in this warmer chamber.

Steam baths were taken in the hot room or *Bayt al-Sajun*. The temperature was kept the hottest here at around 40°C, as this room was situated beside the furnace. Wooden slippers enabled the guests to comfortably walk over the burning-hot floors. The temperature was high enough to ensure that water evaporated when thrown on the floor and would produce a dense cloud of steam. This was the room where most time was spent. Often, the entire process of hot, warm, and cool baths was repeated several times in one day.

The hammam was open and free to the public; mornings were reserved for the men and in the afternoons, the women congregated. The staff of the more luxurious bath houses included professional hairdressers, barbers, masseurs, and perfumers. Cosmeticians, known as *masita*, were also at the disposal of the guests. The women groomed themselves and enjoyed conversations with each other. Massages were offered from oils of almond, apple, jasmine, rose, and water lily. Perfumes and scented oils were highly appreciated by the Spanish Moors, particularly as they were believed to cleanse the mind and heighten the senses. Fragrances such as rose, honeysuckle, orange blossom, musk, jasmine, and oil of violet were often preferred. Beauty products were purchased at the Zoco, such as depilatory items and powdered antimony, or kohl, for the eyes. Kohl was highly popular not only for intensifying the expression but for hygienic purposes, as it was in the days of the ancient Egyptians, who also used *alheña* or henna to color their hair. Henna was mixed with sweet olive oil and was also used to decorate the hands and feet of both men and women with patterns of geometric designs.

Ruins of 13th Century Arab Baths in Ronda

Walking up to the Albayzín and Sacromonte area on *Carrera del Darro* in Granada, you will find *El Bañuelo*, the oldest Arabic bath house in the province and one of the best preserved in the country. Constructed during the rule of Emir *Badis* (1038-1056) of the Zirí Dynasty, it was known to the Moors as *al-Hammam al-Yawza* (Bath of the Walnut). Some of the columns used in its construction were obtained from Roman and Visigoth ruins. Other well-preserved Arab baths in Andalusia can also be found in Ronda (Málaga), and Jaén.

Currently Spain is experiencing a revival of these luxurious baths. Some, built in Granada, Córdoba, and Madrid, have recently opened to the public. The introduction of the Arabic bath is just one of the many wonderful gifts that the Moors brought to Spain, as we shall see in the next chapter.

4. THE GOLDEN AGE

The Islamic conquest of Spain can be regarded as being highly instrumental in the progress and development of a nation praised not only for its achievements, but also for its diversity and tolerance of the communities and people therein. Moorish Spain was not only a time of integration of diverse cultures but of major accomplishments and achievements. During the 9th century, science and technology already began to flourish in al-Andalus. By the 10th century, al-Andalus was prospering as a major cultural, scientific, commercial, and artistic center, illuminated by many brilliant minds.

The 10th century is known as the Golden Age of al-Andalus, as it was then when it achieved its greatest splendor. At this time, Córdoba was the richest, most powerful and advanced state in Western Europe. The population of its capital city of Córdoba at the end of this century is estimated over 500,000; while the population of Almería (27,000), Granada (26,000), Málaga (15,000) and outside Spain; Paris (38,000) and Rome (35,000) lagged quite far behind.

By the 14th century, al-Andalus was the largest state in Europe and was the most advanced and populated center of learning and education. Education was highly valued by the Muslims; public libraries, schools and the first university in Europe were established in al-Andalus. Most Arabs were literate and children attended Koranic schools where boys and girls of the age of six or seven learned how to read, write, recite the Koran and master basic mathematics. Access to the *Madraza* or Islamic school, where the most reputable teachers taught the Koran, medicine, sciences, poetry, grammar, mathematics, and astronomy, was somewhat restricted.

Research institutions and libraries were plentiful and men in quest of higher knowledge came from afar to learn in the universities of al-Andalus. As a result, many great intellectual giants in the form of scientists, physicians, and philosophers emerged. Islamic Spain experienced progress in the fields of alchemy, algebra, agronomy, astrology, astronomy, biology, botany, chemistry, geography, geometry, history, mathematics, medicine, meteorology, navigation, psychology, physics, theology, and zoology.

Córdoba was chosen by Emir *al-Hurr* as the capital and administrative center of al-Andalus in 716, when it so far only occupied Seville. Córdoba quickly developed into the "Jewel of the 10th Century," excelling as a cultural and intellectual center, one of the largest in the world within the Islamic society. It rivaled Baghdad and Constantinople in greatness while serving as the center of Muslim culture and power. Córdoba was a prominent and cultured city where integration between Arabs, Berbers, Jews, and Christians was a reality. Not only was it the thriving capital of al-Andalus but it was also the capital of western Muslims and the greatest city of its time.

At its peak, Córdoba had nearly 30 settled areas outside its city limits. It has been estimated that during its Golden Age there were 100,000 to 200,000 homes, 80,000 merchant shops, 60,000 palaces and estates, 800 public schools, 800 bath houses, 700 mosques, and 50 hospitals. A large hospital was built in Córdoba that had baths with running water. Specialists were assigned to different areas of illness and injuries; it was always open to the public and services were free to the poor.

Leading physicians from al-Andalus include *Ibn Juljul,* born in Córdoba in the year 943; he began his studies at the age of 14 and within a decade became a highly respected and leading physician. Among his achievements were writing commentaries, compiling a list of medicines locally available, and writing a history of Spanish Muslim physicians of al-Andalus.

Ibn Zuhr (also known as *Avenzoar*) was another man of medicine; he was born in Seville in the year 1091. He died in 1161, having earned a reputation not only in al-Andalus but throughout North Africa as one of the greatest physicians of his time. *Ibn al-Khatib* was another noted physician who also excelled in history and poetry. Known as the last of the great men of medicine of al-Andalus, al-Khatib ("the writer," in Arabic) was born in the town of Loja in the province of Granada in the year 1313. He specialized in contagious diseases and authored over 50 books on medicine, poetry, history, music, travel, theology, and politics. Al-Khatib acted as Vizier to Yusuf I and his son Muhammad V. Unfortunately his life took a drastic turn as he was eventually accused of heresy and disloyalty to Muhammad V; he fled to Morocco, where he was assassinated while imprisoned in 1374.

Córdoba also had a university, primary schools, and as many as 50 public libraries. The Umayyads were lovers of literature and therefore collected a great amount of fine works and rare books that they contributed to these libraries. Córdoba was also home to about 70 bookshops and the largest library in the world, with over 500,000 manuscripts collected from other lands in its inventory.

By the beginning of the 11ᵗʰ century, Arabic became the official language of education, state affairs, commerce, culture, and literature. Ambitious intellects and scholars who wished to advance in the world studied Arabic, as this was the language that opened doors to opportunities, much as English is today. It was the language of the literate population, and intellectual thirst produced a stream of illustrious and celebrated thinkers, philosophers, and poets throughout al-Andalus.

Muslims and Jews preserved knowledge by translating the world's finest literature, written by Greek, Persian, Syrian, Egyptian, and other intellectual masters. Jews in particular excelled in translating and Arabs often contributed valuable commentaries in addition to the translations. In Toledo, a school for translators was established during the 12ᵗʰ century where Arabic texts already translated from Greek and Persian were converted into Latin. By the 13ᵗʰ century, Toledo became one of the major cultural centers where scholars, scientists and intellectuals, whether Arab, Jew or Christian, came from afar in their quest for education and higher knowledge.

Many important figures and scholars emerged from al-Andalus such as the lawyer, theologian, philosopher, and great poet Abd al-Hassán Alí Ibn Hazm. Born in Córdoba in 994, he died in Huelva in 1064. Around 1022, Ibn Hazm wrote one of the greatest romantic poems and collection of prose passages, titled, "El Collar de la Paloma," (The Necklace of the Dove). Drawing upon his own experiences and insights, this treatise dealing with the subject of love and lovers is considered to be the finest work of its kind in Arabic literature. Originally titled *Tauq al-Hamamah*, the text was translated into Castilian in 1967 by Emilio García Gómez:

"El Collar de la Paloma"

Por ti tengo celos hasta de que te alcance mi mirada,
Y temo que hasta el tacto de mi mano te disuelva.
Por guardarme de esto, evito encontrarme y
Me propongo unirme contigo mientras duermo.
Así, mi espíritu, si sueño, está contigo,
Separado de los miembros corporales,
Escondido y oculto, pues para unirse contigo,
La unión de las almas es mejor mil veces
Que la unión de los cuerpos...

I am even jealous of my gaze upon you,
And I fear that with the touch of my hand you will fade.
To guard myself from this, I avoid catching myself and
I propose to unite with you while I sleep.
This way, my spirit, if I dream, will be with you,
Separated from our bodily limbs,
Hidden and in secret, for in uniting with you,
The union of the souls is 1000 times greater
Than the union of the bodies...

Another important Muslim scholar (if not the most important), is the writer, philosopher, advisor, physician, judge, mathematician, astronomer, poet, and theologian *Ibn Rushd*, also known as *Avén Ruiz*, but better known as *Averroës*. Born in Córdoba in 1126, Averroës is regarded as the most brilliant Islamic philosopher of all time and even has an asteroid (8318) named in his honor. Averroës came from an educated and influential family; his father and grandfather had been important judges of Córdoba during Almoravid rule. He translated and wrote brilliant commentaries on Aristotle that had great influence not only in the Islamic world but in Christian Europe as well. During the 13th century his works were translated from Arabic into Hebrew. He died in Marrakech during 1198 and his body was transported back to Córdoba to be buried in the family cemetery.

The first outstanding Andalusi physician and surgeon was *Abu al-Qasim al-Zahrawi*, or *Abulcasis*, from Córdoba, born during the 10th century. Al-Zahrawi served as physician to al-Hakam II and compiled a 30-volume medical encyclopaedia known as *Al-Tasrif*. He died in 1013 and his work regarding surgery was never to be surpassed during the Middle Ages.

JEWS OF AL-ANDALUS

By the time the Romans arrived on the Iberian Peninsula, Jewish colonies had already been established. As the most visible minority, they constituted about 1-3% of the population. Thousands more migrated to al-Andalus from Morocco and Egypt during the 8th and 9th centuries. Their population by this time has been estimated at 25,000 and by the 11th century, it more than doubled. By the 12th century the Jewish population of southern Spain surpassed that of Jews in all the other European countries combined.

Under Muslim rule, they were for the first time given the chance to flourish. Spanish Jews greatly prospered, contributing not only culturally but economically, commercially, and scientifically as well. They experienced tolerance, security, freedom, and opportunities to reach high positions within the administration and government of al-Andalus. Possessing shrewd business sense, many worked in small retail shops and excelled as financiers or money lenders. In time, Jewish families came to control maritime commerce. They were the main importers and exporters of Andalusí textiles, leather, silk, spice, fruit, and grain. Many Jews also worked as tailors, tanners, cobblers and jewelers.

Jews were prominent in the fields of science, commerce, astronomy, medicine, administration, and even rose to high positions within the Caliphal Court. *Hasday ibn Shaprut* (914-970) was one such Hebrew scholar. Born in Jaén he worked as a physician and finance minister. As he spoke several languages, he was appointed ambassador to the courts of Abd al-Rahman III. Shaprut also founded schools of medicine and astronomy in Córdoba, Granada, and Toledo.

Al-Andalus boasted the largest and brightest Hebrew community in all of Europe and its citizens were regarded as a highly literate elite. As a result of their language skills, many Jewish scholars served as translators of Arabic texts for Christian Europe, converting thousands of volumes of Muslim translations of classic Greek philosophy into Hebrew and Latin that eventually circulated throughout Europe.

Ibn Ezra, born during the late 11th century, was not only a scholar and rabbi but a master of philosophy, mathematics, geometry, astronomy, and astrology. Ezra authored many books and treatises on these subjects and was also among the first to translate such works from Arabic to Hebrew. His studies and research were based on Persian, Arab, and Hindu astrologers that he properly acknowledged and credited.

Another renowned rabbi was *Musa Ibn Maymun,* or *Moisés ibn Maimónides.* Born in Córdoba (1135-1204) Maimónides, or *Moisés de Maimón,* as he is known to Spaniards, was a brilliant philosopher, physician, and scholar who authored many texts on medicine and Judaism that influenced both the Jewish and non-Jewish worlds. He is regarded as the most influential medieval figure in the field of philosophy.

Jewish scholars also served as mediators between Muslims and Christians. They were respected as advisors, statesmen, doctors, and diplomats to both Muslims and Christians. However, all this came crashing down when Muslim rule weakened and eventually collapsed in southern Spain. By the 13th century, Christians controlled most of the Iberian Peninsula and under the reign of the fanatical Almohads, the Jews were force to adopt the religion of Islam or defend themselves once again from persecution. Although they were generally unsuccessful, one courageous Spanish Jew did rise to the occasion. *Abu Ruiz ibn Dahri* from Granada led a short-lived revolution as the Almohads re-entered Granada. Although his attempt was unsuccessful, it did eventually facilitate the successful campaign, with help from the Jews, that drove the Almohads out of Granada once and for all in 1232.

Two months after the Christians took possession of Granada in 1492, a royal decree was signed to expel all Jews from Spain. Some remained and escaped expulsion by being baptized but the majority refused to convert and went into exile. Those who did outwardly convert to Christianity in order to escape punishment were known as *Conversos;* however, many were executed nevertheless as they were suspected of continuing to be Jews in secret. An estimated 200,000 converted and another 200,000 were forced to leave the country, depriving Spain of their cultural and intellectual contributions and future achievements. This was to become the end of cultural diversity and religious freedom in Spain for centuries to follow.

Those who went into exile were called *Sepharades,* the Hebrew name for Spain. Their language, known as *Ladino,* was a combination of Hebrew and 15th-century Spanish plus many Arabisms; it was written in Hebrew script. This Judo-Spanish language was spoken wherever they settled and it spread throughout the world. Today, Ladino is on a steady decline as fewer than 200,000 people speak the language worldwide; they are mainly based in Israel, the Balkans, and North Africa.

TRADE

The economic structure of al-Andalus was primarily based upon agriculture, mining, fishing, and livestock. The Spanish Moors had the largest merchant marine in the Mediterranean area. Trade prospered here as there was an abundance of commodities in demand that were exported to other lands. From Almería, the main seaport, vessels sailed to the Mediterranean loaded with such goods as dried fruits, timber, saffron, sugar, oil, silks, minerals, and much more. Trade routes passed through Córdoba linking Europe to North Africa and al-Andalus became the major maritime force in the Western world. The Moors introduced the art of glass-making and paper-making to al-Andalus; these flourished as a profitable industry. By the 10th century, Córdoba in particular was highly recognized for its metalwork, leatherwork, ivory goods, weaves, and textiles. Málaga was recognized for pottery work and Granada and Almería were known throughout the Mediterranean region for producing fine silks. Silk weaves and woolen garments were highly appreciated, particularly by the Christian rulers of the north, and constituted the major portion of luxury textiles that were exported — along with others more common textiles, such as cotton, that was also introduced by the Moors. The silks produced in Granada were so admired that after the Reconquest, the Catholic Kings allowed the highly respected industry to carry on. The Moors also manufactured weapons, and more than once the Christian armies used their artillery that was of a higher and more durable quality than any other.

One major export that remains to this day is olive oil. The olive tree was first cultivated here by the Phoenicians and Greeks. However, it was the Romans who significantly expanded oil production and it became an important industry in Spain with new techniques and cultivating methods. Spanish olive oil was highly valued by the people of ancient Rome and today, Italians are its biggest importer — and re-exporter. Upon the fall of the Roman Empire olive production declined throughout the rest of Europe; however, it continued to flourish in southern Spain, with the arrival of the Moors, as they introduced new varieties and superior methods of cultivation.

The Andalusian province of Jaén is recognized as the world's olive oil capital, accounting for 70% of the entire production of Spain. The olive oil of Jaén is regarded throughout the world as the finest in quality.

AGRICULTURE

The Moors introduced a new and improved system of irrigation based on Roman methods that had been neglected by the Visigoths. These methods greatly increased agricultural production, yielding more and better quality crops, many of which were previously unknown to Spain. Most of the country's elaborate irrigation technology of today dates to its Muslim period.

From their homeland the Moors introduced hydraulic wheels known as *norias* that lifted and channeled water directly from a well or river and its tributaries to the vegetable gardens and fields. These were large wheels with buckets driven solely by the force of the water lifted from channels or rivers. The Greeks and Romans also used the hydraulic wheel, but not to the extent of the Moors, who were inspired by the Persians (who excelled in this branch of technology). The other type of water-mill, known as *aceña*, was smaller and was geared by animal or man power. Another system was the use of an irrigation ditch known as *acequia*. All these devices introduced by the Moors not only yielded new crops in al-Andalus but considerably improved and expanded the existing ones.

Vegetables such as eggplants, artichoke, spinach, endives, and wild asparagus were introduced by the Moors as well as many types of fruits that were consumed either fresh, in juice, as a jam, or in desserts. Most of the sweets or desserts in Spain today are of Arabic origin, particularly those with ingredients such as almonds, sugar, honey, nuts, and eggs.

Unknown to Spain prior to the Muslim invasion were sweet oranges, pomegranates, grapes, cherries, coconut palms, dates, figs, olives, peaches, pears, plums, watermelons, bananas, melons, and apricots. The Moors also introduced the almond, sugar-cane and spices such as mint, pepper, coriander, aniseed, nutmeg, parsley, cinnamon, coriander, cumin, and saffron. Saffron and rice are two chief ingredients of Spain's national dish, *paella*.

Viticulture was introduced to al-Andalus by the Phoenicians and was also further developed by the Greeks and Romans. When the Moors arrived, they instituted new distilling methods and increased the number of varieties available. Wine consumption became fashionable in al-Andalus, particularly during the reign of Abd al-Rahman II. Under Roman rule Jeréz de la Frontera in Cádiz and Málaga became major wine-producing centers and they remain so to this day.

ARCHITECTURE

The wonders of architecture scattered throughout Andalusia are glorious visual reminders of the days of long ago, but most importantly, of the greatness achieved by the Muslim civilization of Spain. Many cultures shaped Andalusia but it was the Muslims who left the strongest imprint, particularly in architecture, making it distinct from any other region in Europe. The grandest achievements in al-Andalus were accomplished during the rule of the Caliphate of Córdoba, the Almohad Kings of Seville and the Nasrid Dynasty of Granada.

Christian architecture was highly influenced by Islamic design and construction. Two styles of art and architecture developed from the union of Arabs and Christians is exclusive to Spain. These styles are known as *Mudéjar* and *Mozárabic*. Mudéjar arose from the Muslims that remained in Christian Spain after the Reconquest and Mozárabic arose from the Christians living in Muslim Spain, particularly throughout the northern regions. Mudéjar architecture dates from the 11th to the 16th century and is much more common throughout the peninsula than the older Mozarabic, which was used from the 9th to 11th century.

Among the greatest architectural legacies of the Spanish Moors are indeed the Alhambra palace fortress of Granada and the mosque in Córdoba. In Seville stands another landmark: the 12th century *Giralda Tower* or former Almohad minaret that once stood as an astronomical observatory. It was built under the supervision of the mathematician and astronomer *Jabir ibn Aflah* of Seville.

ASTRONOMY/ASTROLOGY

Astrology was regarded by many as a science closely linked to astronomy and mathematics; as such it was held in high regard. The Arabs were highly advanced in these areas and operated on the belief that the motions of celestial bodies affect life on earth and that by studying their movements, one could predict coming events. They made tremendous contributions to the science of astronomy, particularly during the 10th century. Many of the bright stars are still known by a version of their Arabic name, such as Betelgeuse (from *Yad al-Jawza*, or "Hand of Orion"), Aldebaran (from *al-Dabaran*, or "Follower of the Pleiades"), Suhail (from *al-Suhail*, translating as "The Plain") and Fomalhaut (from *Fum al-Hut*, or "Mouth of the Fish"), to name a few. However, the Arabs were not always the first to name these stars as the ancient Egyptians, Greeks and Romans had also been active in this sphere.

The Arabs built exceptional observatories and developed meticulous astronomical instruments intended to achieve accuracy in the calculation and observation of celestial bodies. Astronomical calculations were also used in architecture as the construction of buildings had to be aligned in the direction of Mecca.

During the reign of Abd al Rahman II there lived one gifted astrologer, poet, music teacher, and alchemist of the Caliphal courts of Córdoba. His name was *Abbas ibn Firnas* (?- 888). Born in Ronda (Málaga), Firnas was learned in mathematics, physics, chemistry, and astronomy; he compiled tables of planetary motions. Firnas was creative and multi-talented. He gained a reputation as an eccentric sage due to his numerous curious hobbies, inventions, and contraptions. Among his many accomplishments, he designed and built a mechanized planetarium with revolving planets, a water clock, and an armillary sphere, and devised a method for producing artificial crystals. Firnas is believed to have introduced glass-making techniques to al-Andalus. Perhaps his most curious invention or experiment was the construction of a flying machine, with which he attempted to fly using a pair of feathered wings inside a wooden frame. Today, he has not only an airport in Baghdad named in his honor but a lunar crater as well.

Astrology was popular among the Muslim rulers of Spain and continued to flourish during the 11th century. The Umayyad rulers often kept an official stargazer within their courts. *Yusuf ibn Ahmad Al-Mu'tamin* of Zaragoza was a skilled astrologer who was believed to have correctly predicted his own death in 1085. *Muhammad ibn Abbad Al-Mu'tamid* (1040-1095), the poet king of Seville, frequently consulted a Jewish rabbi and astrologer from Córdoba for stellar wisdom and advice.

Tables or *zîjât* were used in the calculation of planetary motions, declinations and eclipses, and armillary spheres consisting of a hollow orb with a series of circles that turned upon its polar axis. Sophisticated astrolabes were designed and used to determine latitudes, the time of day and night and the motion of the sun, stars and signs of the zodiac in order to observe the sky and calculate predictive events. The Hellenic astrolabe was simplified during the 11th century by a leading mathematician and astronomer named *al-Zarqali*. Born in Toledo (1029-1087), he was also known as *Azarquiel*. His improved version remained in use until the 16th century. Azarquiel constructed many instruments for astronomical research and calculations. He comprised an almanac, tables of latitude and longitude, and the famous *Toledan Tables* as well that were based upon his observations in Toledo during the second half of the 11th century. His work improved the casting of astrological charts that were becoming quite popular within political fields and the Caliphal courts. Azarquiel is regarded as the foremost Spanish/Muslim astronomer of his time; his works were meticulously studied by Western scholars. Also during the 11th century, mathematician and astronomer *Ibn al-Saffar* from Córdoba comprised astronomical tables and wrote a short but valuable treatise on the use of the astrolabe.

However, the original and leading authority or master in mathematics, astronomy and astrology was the great scholar *Máslama ibn Ahmad al-Majriti*. He was born in Madrid (c. 950-c. 1008), then known as *Majerit*. His name provides the first reference to Spain's present capital that was during his time nothing more than a small settlement.

Máslama wrote an enormous quantity of works on these subjects as well as on magic, talismans, witchcraft, and alchemy. He believed that all these subjects were related and that alchemy (from Arabic *al-kimia*, meaning "the hidden" or "the occult") was derived from science and philosophy. Máslama wrote treaties on mathematics and astronomy and introduced the concept of "zero" to al-Andalus. He also corrected, revised, and expanded the astronomical tablets written by renowned Persian scientist and mathematician *al-Kwarizmi* two centuries earlier. During the early 11th century, Máslama founded a school of mathematics and astronomy as he became well known for his accurate astrological predictions.

Máslama also served as the astrological counselor to al-Mansur, whom he often advised on the condition of the stars and planets, whether they were auspicious or detrimental, before beginning an expedition or important campaign. It is believed that al-Mansur did not initiate any campaigns without first consulting his personal astrologer. Máslama died in Córdoba and is believed to have predicted the political upheaval that took place shortly after his death.

Abd Allah, Taifa king of Granada and firm believer in astrology, credited astrology for the success and victories of al-Mansur that were predicted by his horoscope. Abd Allah wrote an extensive defense of astrology, calling it a form of worship and stating that man was able to ponder God's creation through the astrolabe.

There is an interesting legend about an 11th century Moorish king of Granada named *ibn Habus al-Badise* (or *Badis Aben Habuz*), who with the help of an Arabian astrologer and sage was able to crush approaching enemies. Each day the king grew increasingly worried about the state of his defense and began taking extra precautions by securing the mountainous countryside where enemies could easily attack. He built watchtowers along the mountains and stationed guards who alerted the king with fire and smoke signals when danger approached. Nevertheless he remained troubled, feeling vulnerable and somewhat dissatisfied with these methods.

Then to his aid arrived in Granada an aged Arabian sage from the East, who claimed to have walked from the land of Egypt with the help of a walking stick inscribed with hieroglyphs. The wise man's name was *Ibrahim ibn abu Ajib;* his father was a close friend of the Prophet Muhammad. As a child, Ibrahim studied with the priests of Egypt for many years and grew to become wise in the ways of magic and sorcery. The king quickly took to the astrologer and offered him to stay at his palace — which he refused, as he much preferred to humbly live in a cave on the hill where the Alhambra now stands today.

It wasn't long before Ibrahim was consulted on every emergency that the distraught king faced. The sage quickly became most indispensable with his astrological charts, talismans, and potions. Ibrahim began to tell the king of a device that was used in ancient Egypt that alerted them to impending invasions, in the form of a brass rooster and ram that turned on a pivot. The astonishing thing about it was that the rooster would crow and the ram turned upon the pivot facing the direction of the enemies when they approached. Immediately the king ordered this device to be crafted for his protection, in exchange for all the riches and rewards the sage requested for his cave.

The magician began his work at once and constructed a tower on top of the palace where access was for forbidden to all except the king and astrologer. Inside the tower, miniature battles scenes with wooden horses and soldiers were constructed and placed upon small tables before each window. Above the tower was positioned a bronze Moorish horseman figure on a pivot holding a shield and spear. The face of this figure was directed towards the city as if guarding it; however, if danger approached, the face of the figure would turn towards the direction of the danger while his spear would rise as in battle.

Anxious to see the results, the king and astrologer were soon satisfied. Almost immediately they were alerted that the face of the bronze horseman had turned in the direction of the mountains. Upon hearing the news, they dashed up the staircase to the tower and saw the miniature wooden figures upon the board moving about as if in battle. This was all the proof they needed and the astrologer told the king to strike the figures with his magical staff. In an instant the king plunged the lance down hard onto the table of the wooden effigies, completely destroying it.

The king quickly sent forth his men to the mountainous area to confirm the attack and destruction. Soon the soldiers returned to the palace with news of an army of Christian men who had been approaching through the mountains. They discovered that quite suddenly and inexplicably the Christian soldiers had turned their weapons against each other and retreated, as if disoriented and confused, across the border to their homes.

The Founder of Andalusí Music

During the 9th and 10th centuries, Andalusí literature, poetry and prose flourished, particularly one style of poetic compositions formulated in classical Arabic known as *Muwashaha* or *Moaxaja*. Both Spanish Muslims and Christians particularly appreciated the compositions developed by a blind Spanish/Arab poet named *El Cabrí* (from Córdoba, he lived during the 9th century). An example of this poetic form, exclusive to Moorish Spain, is the traditional 10th century Andalusí song *Lamma Bada.* Many versions of this song have been composed but *Radio Tarifa* performs a haunting version of this classic with a superb blend of Spanish, Moorish, and Sephardic musical styles.

The *Zéjel* or *Zayal* was another popular form in colloquial Arabic that developed from the Moaxajas, as were the *Jarchas*, poems expressing the joys and sorrows of love. Jarchas were verses written by Arabic and Hebrew poets in Arabic or Hebrew script in the Romance dialect of Mozárabic that was popular during the 10th and 11th centuries. It is actually the first form of written poetry or lyrical compositions to develop in Spain. The Jarchas consisted of two to four stanzas, generally written for the female voice that appeared at the end of Moaxajas:

> Amanu, ya habibi,
> Al-wahs me no farás.
> Ben, beza mia bokella,
> Awsak tú no irás!

> Believe me, my love,
> You will not leave me all alone.
> Come, kiss my little mouth,
> And I know that you will not go!

The Zéjel and the Moaxaja experienced their peak in popularity between the 11th and 13th centuries and they exist as the two major contributions of al-Andalus to the field of poetry.

Moorish singing and dancing slave girls known as *Qiyân* (singular *Qayna*), who accompanied their performance with percussion musical instruments, were quite popular and highly respected by Moorish Spain society. Many were brought into Rome to perform for high society. According to medieval chronicles, the Qiyan were beautiful women with magnificent voices who were trained in the classic schools of the Orient. They were regarded as women of perfection, seduction, servitude, elegance, talent, and rhythm. These singers also recited poetry and were highly literate and articulate. They wore the finest jewelry and perfumes of the rarest essences. Few records remain to indicate how they were compensated, although there is one account stating that during the reign of al-Hakam I a Qayna named *Aziz* was purchased for 10,000 dirhams; and there is documentation stating that they were rewarded with precious jewels and fines silks.

During the reign of the first Umayyad emir, Abd al-Rahman I, many such oriental singers arrived in Córdoba from the classic schools of their homeland. One in particular that the Emir purchased was a female singing slave from Medina named *Ayfâ*. Many more were to follow, especially during the rule of Abd al-Rahman II, who went as far as to dedicate one of his palaces to the singers; it is known as *Dar al-Madaniyyat* or "Home of the Girls from Medina."

During the 9th century, determined to be superior in every way to the rivaling court of the Baghdad Caliphate, Abd al-Rahman II recruited many historians, philosophers, scholars and poets to al-Andalus. Singers and musicians were also in high demand and they went forth from Baghdad to entertain the nobility of al-Andalus. The music of Persia was highly advanced and had been integrating with that of its ancient neighboring India for centuries.

One such musical scholar, gifted singer, poet, court musician and composer born in Mesopotamia was named *Ziryab* (789-857). Ziryab performed for the famous Abbasid court of the Caliph *Harun al-Rashid* in Baghdad, who is believed to be the Caliph in the tales of "*A Thousand and One Nights*" or "*Arabian Nights.*"

Ziryab was invited to al-Andalus by al-Hakam I. When he arrived at the port of Algecíras in 822, he immediately presented himself in Córdoba and was welcomed by Abd al-Rahman II. The invitation came at a most opportune time when Ziryab was experiencing difficulties due to increasing jealousy, rumors, and threats spread by his former musical teacher, *Ishaq al-Mawsili,* in Baghdad. It was the right time and place for Ziryab to arrive and culturally "conquer" al-Andalus. Here Ziryab had an opportunity that he could not pass up, a playground for his musical ideas and talents.

Ziryab

Born *Abd-al-Hasan Ali-ibn-Nafi*, Ziryab was a remarkable Kurdish singer, musician, composer and courtier and, like Firnas, had many interests and hobbies. His nickname "Ziryab" means "blackbird" or "black nightingale," and referred to his dark complexion and falsetto singing voice. He settled in the town of Córdoba and immediately became the chief musician of the Royal Court in the 9th century.

As a brilliant scholar, Ziryab introduced al-Andalus to his innovative ideas in philosophy, astronomy, astrology, and medicine. He was also renowned for his knowledge in geography and excelled as a poet and conversationalist. In political decisions, Ziryab was frequently consulted as he recommended structural changes within government administration.

He quickly became the toast of the town and a favorite among the elite. His creative influences spread throughout Western Europe and beyond and his innovations set the trends for centuries to follow. Hairstyles of Andalusí medieval aristocracy were influenced by his artistic sense as he introduced new and daring styles that were frequently imitated. It is believed that he established a type of tunic or gown with narrow sleeves that became the standard dress of both men and women. It was Ziryab who was responsible for setting fashion trends in al-Andalus, such as wearing bright colors of wool, cotton and linen fabrics in the spring, white during the hot summer months, darker colors and cloaks trimmed with fur of rabbit, lamb or weasel for the fall or colder winter months. Ziryab opened a cosmetology school for women and introduced new methods of etiquette and style. He is also responsible for bringing elegant tableware, crystal glasses, exotic recipes, leather furniture, fine cosmetics, and toiletries such as toothpaste, deodorant, and perfumes from the East, as well as introducing the games of polo and chess to al-Andalus. Ziryab also popularized the consumption of wine.

Often accompanying himself with a lute, Ziryab is known to have strummed and sung thousands of songs that he knew by memory. His innovative ideas inspired him to modify the lute by adding a fifth bass string; this instrument eventually evolved into the Spanish guitar. He also introduced the idea of using a plectrum made from the talons of an eagle that replaced the wooden ones that were previously used.

Ziryab is credited with setting the standards of written rules regarding the interpretation of the *Nouba* or *Nawbah*, the Andalusí form of North African music that remains a significant and authentic music tradition of Morocco, Tunisia, and Algeria. Today's renowned guitarist Paco de Lucía named one of his albums after him.

In 822 Ziryab established the first music conservatory, or more likely school, in Córdoba. Ziryab prepared over 30 young women to become Qiyan, including two of his own daughters, and another two that became the favorites of Abd al-Rahman II. He introduced Persian and Hindu modes to

Andalusí music and rhythms. Ziryab's new musical methods influenced European medieval music. He is regarded as the father of Andalusí music as he established the musical traditions of Moorish Spain and laid the foundation for what was to become, centuries later, the cultural signature and greatest achievement of the next wave of people that migrated to Spain in search of a better life.

5. The Gypsies

About a thousand years ago groups of people left their homes in the Punjabi region of northern India and Sindh, the southern province of Hindustan now known as Pakistan, in several waves of migration. They were so many in number that they divided themselves into groups. Escaping imprisonment during the Turk-Persian invasion of their home regions, they wandered westward through Afghanistan, Persia, Turkey, Syria, Egypt, and North Africa.

During the 12th century many tribes divided and migrated to what are now the Eastern European countries of Romania, Hungary, Slovakia, and Poland. By the 15th century many Gypsy tribes settled further into Western Europe in such countries as England, France, and as far south as Spain. Some are believed to have entered the Iberian Peninsula from the northern shores of Africa over the Straits of Gibraltar and others entered northern Spain through France via the Pyrenees Mountains. The *Annales de Cataluña*, the first documented record of Gypsies entering Spain, dates as far back as 1447 when they arrived at Barcelona. However, there is earlier evidence dating to 1425 of Gypsies entering through the Pyrenees and settling in Zaragoza, the capital of Aragón. It wasn't until 1462 that they arrived in Andalusia.

Family tribes traveled in groups of 40 to 100 that were led by a "Duke" or "Count." The Gypsies, or *Beticos*, as they were known, were particularly drawn to Andalusia where they discovered a fertile ground for the development of their music and dance, influenced as it was by a rich cultural history and remnants of compatible oriental traditions already established by the Moors during eight centuries as well as those of the Jewish population, both excelling in music and poetry. The music of southern Spain is different from that of any other country that the Gypsies inhabited due to these Moorish musical influences. Another factor regarding the attraction towards southern Spain was the warm climate; but more importantly, the tradition of greater tolerance of different people and cultures was a welcome contrast to what Gypsies experienced elsewhere; they found it easy to assimilate and settle in Andalusia.

The Moriscos and newly arrived Gypsies integrated as best as they could in Andalusia, sharing not only physical features such as dark hair and skin tone but notably their sense of oppression as well. As a traveling people, Gypsy families brought their culture, habits, music, and dance wherever they settled, absorbing the rudiments of whatever local culture was already established and embellishing it with their own styles. When the Gypsies arrived in Andalusia, their Hindi musical system and dance styles fused well with the local Andalusian and Arabic influences.

Of all the Spanish regions, Andalusia, as it was known as after the Reconquest, was the area most populated by the Gypsies. Unfortunately for them, they arrived at a more oppressive period when all Moors and Jews were being persecuted and punished by the Catholic Church for not sharing their religious beliefs.

Music has always been an important aspect of Gypsy culture and traces of their song and dance remain throughout the lands where they traveled. For example the tribes of the *Ghawazee* (Outsiders) of Egypt, the *Romanie* of Eastern Europe, and the *Çingene* of Turkey are all celebrated for their different styles of dance and music, all being of Rom origin. Many believe that here lie the roots of oriental dance as well.

The Gypsies of Spain are heirs of an art form without academic training and are masters of improvisation. Music and dance have always been an emotional release, a means of escape, to them, releasing pressure, and vocalizing intense emotions. The Gypsies found a way to share their joys and sorrows and they express themselves through their music and dance. A film that has captured the essence of the universal hardships and travels of the Gypsies is *Latcho Drom*, meaning "Safe Journey." Written and directed by Tony Gatlif (who is of Gypsy heritage), this documentary has no dialogue or "acting," but tells through music and dance the story of their migration through the Middle East and Europe.

The film opens with Gypsies leaving their home in Rajasthan and progressing in their horse-drawn caravans through Egypt, Turkey, Romania, Hungary, Slovakia, France, and finally Spain. Their hardships and pain is passionately conveyed through their music wherever they traveled.

In Spain, there are two kinds of Gypsies; *Gitanos* (Gypsies) and *Húngaros* (Hungarians). Húngaros, also known as *Zíngaros*, are the *Kalderash* Roma from central Europe who migrated to Spain. They can be of lighter hair and skin tone due to integration with Europeans over the centuries. Traditionally, they are pot (*Kelderara*) makers who consider themselves to be the only authentic Gypsies. The Kalderash were much poorer, living their nomadic lifestyles in tents, huts, and even abandoned cars outside the larger cities. Spaniards regard Húngaros as Gypsies while many Gypsies consider it an insult to be associated with Húngaros.

The Spanish Gypsies were somewhat more sedentary than their east European counterparts in the sense that they actually settled in Andalusia and became less nomadic. Today however, very few Spanish Gypsies actually live a traveling lifestyle.

The Gypsies of Seville are known as *Flamencos* and those from Granada are called *Gitanos*. All Spanish Gypsies refer to non-Gypsies as *Payos*, often in a slightly derogatory manner, and *Castellanos* in an appreciative sense. "Payo" is a Castilian word derived from *Pelayo* or *pagés* (Catalan for "farmer" or "countryman") that is often used by Gypsies to identify those who are not Gypsy. However, from the Gypsy language comes the other deprecating term for a non-Gypsy; *gachó* for a male and *gachí* for a female. These terms are derived from the Romani word *gadjo*, meaning "foreigner" or "non-Gypsy." In the everyday language of Castilian, the depreciative terms "gachó" and "gachí" are also used by Spanish non-Gypsies to describe anybody, Gypsy or not, as uncouth or unrefined. The term "Gypsy," which I believe should be capitalized, is outdated as they are now known worldwide as *Rom*, *Roma* or *Romani*. However, I refer to the Spanish Rom as "Gitanos" or "Gypsies," as they are still known throughout Spain. Interestingly, the Romani word for "husband" is *Rom* and its plural form is *Roma*.

The Roma of Spain are known as *Calé*, from the Hindi *kâlâ*, or "black," referring to their darker skin tone. Their Romani language, based on the ancient Hindi Sanskrit, is known as *Caló* (derived from *Zincaló* meaning "the black men"). Few speak this language today, which survives only in the song of the Gypsies and in Spanish slang. Some examples of this Andalusian dialect in the everyday use of Castilian are *chungo* (to be unwell) and *chaláo* (to be crazy). Like the language of Ladino, it is generally easy for a Castilian to understand Caló; however, there are many differences as well. Many Flamenco songs are sung in Caló, but since the 19th century the language has rarely been used. Below is a list of words frequently heard in Flamenco songs, and their translations, in order to illustrate these dissimilarities:

Caló	Castilian	**English**
Acais	Ojos	Eyes
Sorí	Alegría	Joy
Barí	Bueno	Good
Camelar	Amar	To love
Garlochí	Corazón	Heart
Orchí	Alma	Soul
Quelo	Baile	Dance
Singa	Canción	Song
Ulaque	Fiesta	Party
Monró	Amigo	Friend
Parné	Dinero	Money

The Gypsies of Spain have their own jargon or slang based on Caló, known as *Germanía*, that is used primarily among thieves to keep outsiders in the dark. The Catalonian term is derived not from the name of the European country but from the Castilian word *hermandad*, meaning "brotherhood."

Of major importance to the Gypsies are their family, heritage, and ancestry. As they are quite fond of music and dance, weddings are celebrated in the grandest manner lasting as long as three days or more. Most marriages are arranged to create a bond between two Gypsy families or clans.

The night before the wedding and after the banquet, the most important ceremony is performed. The bride must undergo a ritual performed by the eldest female member of the family, with a white handkerchief that will indicate whether she is "pure" or not. If she does not pass the test, the groom has the right to cancel the wedding. If the test is passed, the spotted handkerchief is shown to everyone's great delight.

Ceremonial games are played within the festivities, such as the bride being kidnapped by the groom on the wedding day. The ransom is to be paid by the groom's family to the family of the bride as compensation for the loss of their daughter before the festivities begin; all done in good humor and fun. A superstitious Gypsy tradition is to smash a pitcher and count how many pieces there are. The number of broken pieces represents the number of years of happiness expected for the newlywed couple.

On the day of the wedding, at sunrise, the bride is crowned and the festivities begin. Once they are married and the newlyweds appear, the guests shower them with aniseed and almonds for good luck and encouragement for dancing. As in all Gypsy festivities, singing, dancing and music as an expression of joy and happiness are at its core. That is captured in the old song *La Tani* written by Genaro Monreal:

A la cueva que hay en Graná ha llegado de tierra lejana
Como reina en carroza dorá, una niña princesa gitana.
Tani le llaman de nombre, es más bonita que un sol.
No camela corona real, y camela un gitano español.
Los blancos pañuelos la rosa tendrá, que no hay otra novia más
    guapa y honrá.

Ay Tani, Tani, mi Tani, Ay Tani, Tani mi Tá
Ay Tani, Tani, morena que corre en tus venas la sangre real.
Ay Tani, que mi Tani, que mi Tani, ay Tani que mi Tani, que mi Tá
Ay Tani, Tani, morena, gitana más buena no ha habido ni habrá

Hoy los novios se van a casar donde tiene su trono la Zambra.
Y la boda se va a celebrar en el patio mejor de la Alhambra
Llegan del tol mundo entero, la caravana Calé...
Y la palma de rumba le dan a La Isla, Triana y Jeréz

At the caves that are found in Granada, from a land far away has
    arrived
Like a queen in a golden carriage, a young gypsy princess.
Tani is her name, she is lovelier than a sun.
Her heart is not set on any royal crown, her heart is set upon a
    Spanish Gypsy man.
Her white handkerchief, the rose will show
There is no other bride more lovely and honorable.

Ay Tani, Tani, mi Tani, Ay Tani, Tani mi Tá
Ay Tani, Tani, dark beauty, royal blood flows through your veins.
Ay Tani, que mi Tani, que mi Tani, ay Tani que mi Tani, que mi Tá
Ay Tani, Tani, dark Gypsy lass, there's never been anyone lovelier
than you and never will there be.

Today the couple will wed where they have their throne at the
Zambra
And the wedding will be celebrated at the finest court of the
Alhambra.
Arriving from all over the world is the caravan of Gypsies
And they clap to the rumba of La Isla, Triana and Jeréz.

When the Gypsies came to Spain, some made a living by resorting to begging and thieving, including highway robbery, while others were able to hold down jobs — somewhat blending into society. The Gypsies that settled down took up such traditional jobs such as horse dealing, animal training, farming, shearing, bread-making, metal-working, leather-working, tailoring, shoemaking, dancing, music, acrobatics, and some even became craftsmen to the Christian army. However, the traditional or most popular craft of the Gypsies was that of a blacksmith. The Gypsies also made brass or copper pots and woven baskets. The "basket weavers" were known as *canasteros*, from the Spanish word *canasta* meaning "basket."

Fortunetelling and healing were other means of earning a living, particularly for the Gypsy women. Gitanas told fortunes by means of tarot card reading and palmistry. Their image was murky and mysterious as they allowed it to be understood that they were in tune with higher powers. This was encouraged by the myth that they came from Little Egypt and brought with them the occult knowledge of the ancient Egyptians. The Gypsies themselves promoted this belief as it added to their mystique and fascination, enabling them to earn a better living through fortune-telling.

Two seasoned Gitanas and former well-known Flamenco dancers correctly predicted my own father's fortune in 1934 when he lived in Seville. "*Jóven!*" they would call out to him, "*Ven aqui que te eche la buenaventura!* (Youngster, come here so we can tell you your fortune!) The Gitanas, who lived in the same building and on the same floor as my father, intimated him as a young boy of 14 years old. He remembers how they quickly hid their lit cigarettes behind their backs when he walked passed them. "*Las Serranas*," as they were professionally known, had performed as far away from their homeland as New York City.

One day they took my father's hand and began reading his palm. "You will survive a war, later move to America, and live a long life," said the Gypsy women. And a few years later, my father fought in the Spanish civil war. He immigrated to North America in the sixties, and is currently quite healthy at 87 years of age. After telling his fortune, my father recalls that the Gypsies did not ask him for money.

Yolanda Ramos sings about the Gypsies and their reputation for telling fortunes by means of card-reading in her song "Quiero saber mi suerte (*Échame las Cartas*)," written and composed by Vicente Castro.

> En por la parte de la isla dicen que hay una gitana
> Que al curar los desengaños solo con verte la cara.
> Mañana por la mañana encuantito me levante
> Voy a ver esa gitana porque va curar mis males.
> Échame las cartas
> Que quiero saber mi suerte
> Si ese gitano me ama.

> On one side of the island they say there's a Gypsy woman
> Who can heal your sorrows just by looking at your face.
> Tomorrow in the morning as soon as I awake
> I will go see that Gypsy as she will cure my misfortunes.
> Tell me what the cards say
> I want to know my fortune
> Does that Gypsy man love me?

SACROMONTE

Gitanos in Granada made their homes in the caves dug into the *Sacromonte Hill* that rises behind the old Arab residential quarter of *Albayzín* in front of the Alhambra.

The walls of the caves are a product of deposits consisting of a mixture of mud, round pebbles, and rocks that have shifted and fossilized since their original creation approximately eight million years ago. These caves became the sacred homes of the Spanish Gypsies who arrived over 500 years ago. During the last half century, the cave dwellings have been improved to resemble comfortable middle class homes, with modern plumbing and electricity. The interiors are brightly decorated with cooking utensils and countless brass plates that are hung upon the white walls and ceilings.

The Gypsies of the Sacromonte still put on their shows or *Zambras* to the general public. The caves mainly serve as tourist venues for these performances. Chairs are lined up along the side of both walls of the long and narrow cave and here the audience can participate, when encouraged by the performers, being much more intimate and up close as opposed to larger theatre or stage settings. The final part of the show involves interaction with audience members that are selected individually for a quick improvised lesson — to the delight and amusement of all. At the *Cueva de la Maria La Canastera* I was selected from the audience one memorable night in 2002.

Sacromonte, Granada

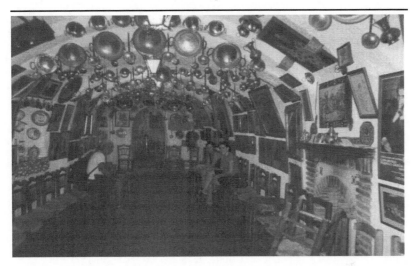

Cueva de Maria La Canastera in Sacromonte

As a student of Flamenco, I had some idea of what I was being coached to do, a few steps here and a few steps there and I was able to follow the dancer. Dancing with the Gypsies of Granada, even if for a brief moment, certainly injected a sense of "magic" into the dance for me.

Of all the caves, the late Maria La Canastera's is the most famous. Born María Cortés Heredia, in 1913, she was among one of the first performers to emerge in the Sacromonte area. She appeared in a film starring Pastora Imperio and Carmen Amaya titled *Maria de la O* in 1936. In one scene, a very young Carmen Amaya performs at a Zambra in Sacromonte with the Alhambra towering behind at a distance. She is surrounded by a large circle of Gitanas that include Maria La Canastera who encourage Amaya to express herself through dance. Amaya immediately throws herself into a defiant and thunderous tacóneo as she claps and furiously finger snaps to the rhythm and counter-rhythm of the music. Manipulating her skirt, taking us from one extreme to the other, from slow and mesmerizing sways to fast and sharp heelwork and spins, she is a tornado of fiery energy. When the performance is over, Amaya walks away visibly exhausted and joins the rest of the Gitanas, who joyfully dance to the popular Gypsy song, "*La Mosca.*"

Maria La Canastera was not only recognized as the leader of her clan but as Empress of a Gypsy tribe. Her particular cave is unique from the others as it doubles as a Flamenco and Zambra museum during the day. Her surviving son Enrique takes you through a tour of his mother's home as it is preserved in its original, somewhat eerie state while he offers you a glass of wine that is included in the ticket price. The walls of the cave where her five children were born and raised are filled with mementos of Flamenco's history. This includes many photographs of international celebrities who have visited such as Anthony Quinn, Ingrid Bergman, Yul Brynner, Henry Fonda, Glenn Ford, and Claudia Cardinale.

Nowadays, the performers do not actually live in the caves of Sacromonte anymore. They own apartments in the city while most of the caves have been bought and turned into holiday homes by European visitors.

During the 15th century the Gypsies, like the Morerías of the Moors and Juderías of the Jews, had their own exclusive neighborhoods or districts called *Gitanerías* established in such cities as Granada, Seville, Jeréz, and Cádiz. The Gitanerías likely arose from the laws imposed upon the Gypsies to abandon their wandering lifestyle and settle down in one particular area or else suffer the penalty of deportation or death. The Gitanerías were secretly visited during the evenings by Payos where Gypsies entertained them by dancing and singing under the illuminating light of the moon.

"Bulerías" by Manuel Ruiz, 1960

However, it wasn't long before the Gypsies began being persecuted and ostracized for their lack of religion and common values, failure to contribute to society, and their highly questionable lifestyle, once again becoming victims of discrimination. The Gypsies refused to conform to the customs and laws of society of the countries that they settled in. As the Jewish minorities began leaving Spain, the Gypsies, who previously had been more or less ignored by the Catholic Kings, came into focus. In 1499, harsh laws were imposed by King Fernando and Queen Isabella upon the Gypsies that were to persist until the late 18th century as each new ruler enforced anti-Gypsies laws upon the community.

The Gypsies were prohibited from traveling in groups of more than two. They were denied legal rights or the right to own property and were even limited as to the number allowed to settle in a certain area. They were forbidden to work as blacksmiths, their most traditional occupation. If they failed to accept all this, they had to the leave the country. On March 4, 1499, the first edict against the Gypsies was issued in a small town known as *Medina del Campo*. It stated that if they did not comply within 60 days they would have to face permanent exile from Spain. Three years later, all Gypsies who did not convert to Christianity were forced to emigrate.

El Lebrijano recorded a song in the late 1970s that emotively and accurately narrates the story of their persecution. It is found on his appropriately titled album, "Persecución," that contains texts from the great poet Félix Grande from Badajoz.

Ay, Ay, ay!
No fueron los judíos ni los moros,
Fueron los reyes cristianos, ella se llamó Isabel el se llamaba
  Fernando
Cuando firmaron la ley no les temblaron las manos

Finales del siglo XV, noventa y nueve era el año
Una ley sin compasión nace en Medina del Campo
Cuando firmó, firmó la ley, no les tembló, tembló la mano.

La vieja miel del camino se convierte en miedo amargo
Y la vieja libertad cierra el siglo tiritando.

Mando, mando que en sesenta días a partir de hoy contados
Abandonen los caminos y dejen de ser gitanos
Abandonen sus carretas (y dejen de ser gitanos)
Abandonen sus costumbres (y dejen de ser gitanos)
Se conviertan en sirvientes (y dejen de ser gitanos)
Renieguen su libertad (y dejen de ser gitanos)."

Majestades, majestades,

Doña Isabel, Don Fernando
Antes de poner la firma pensarlo, por Dios, pensarlo!

"Mando que si no obedecen se les den cien latigazos
Y con sangre en la espalda del reino sean desterrados
Y por la segunda vez, con cuchillos afilados
Que les corten las orejas y vuelvan otra vez a ser desterrados
Y por la tercera vez, si no cumplen lo mandado
Que les apresen y que sea por toda la vida ya esclavos."

Finales del siglo XV, noventa y nueve era el año
Toda España nos persiguen desde Medina del Campo
Narremos muchos siglos, siglos de sangre y de espanto
Narremos muchos siglos pa seguir siendo gitanos...

Ay, ay, ay!
It was not the Jews nor was it the Moors
It was the Christian rulers, her name was Isabel and his was
    Fernando
When they signed the law their hands did not tremble
At the end of the 15th century, ninety-nine was the year
A law without compassion was born in Medina del Campo.

*The sweet old ways of the journey have given way to bitter fear.
And the old freedom closes the century shivering.

"I declare that in 60 days as of today
They shall abandon their ways and no longer be Gypsies
They shall abandon their wagons (and no longer be Gypsies)
They shall abandon their customs (and no longer be Gypsies)
They shall become servants (and no longer be Gypsies)
And forsake their freedom (and no longer be Gypsies)."

Your majesty, your majesty, Lady Isabel and Sir Fernando
Before signing this law, think it over, by God, think again!

"I declare and proclaim that if they do not obey, give them 100
    lashes,
And with blood on their backs from the Kingdom they shall be
    banished.
And the second time with sharpened knives,
Their ears shall be cut off and again shall be banished.
And on the third time if they do not obey the orders,
They shall be imprisoned and for the rest of their lives be
    enslaved."

> At the end of the 15ᵗʰ century, ninety-nine was the year
> That all of Spain persecuted us from Medina del Campo.
> We shall tell of many centuries, centuries of blood and horror
> We shall tell of many centuries but will go on forever being
> Gypsies...

In 1525 a law was renewed in Toledo specifying that Gypsies who were apprehended the third time for their vagabond lifestyle were to serve as slaves for the remainder of the lives to their captors. In 1538 King Carlos I renewed the law of Medina del Campo prohibiting the Gypsies from traveling or wandering within the land with such harsh penalties as 100 lashes, the amputation of ears, being chained for 60 days, and enslavement. His son Felipe II was to follow in his footsteps, renewing these edicts in 1586 and prohibiting the language and manner of dress of the Gypsies for the purpose of obliterating the memory of their lifestyle and culture. One wonders what was the success rate; in 1619, Felipe III again prohibited the wearing of their typical clothing and use of their language. Years later, in 1633, during the reign of Felipe IV, an edict was published denying the existence of the Gypsy race as a specific and unique culture, stating that "Gitano" was merely a word describing a delinquent and vagabond way of life.

It wasn't until 1782 that Carlos III revoked some of the laws imposed upon the Gypsies of Spain that had a lasting impact. However, certain conditions had to be met. The Gypsies were still prohibited from using their language and manner of dress, and maintaining their wandering lifestyle, but they were now able to hold whatever legal or honest trade or labor they sought and to settle in any community without prejudice.

King Carlos III was known for his tolerance and he issued new edicts that gave rights to the Gypsies as long as they conformed to the general laws. He was responsible for initiating the slow process of successfully integrating the Gypsies of Spain into society. For the first time, they were placed as near-equals with the rest of the population. They began to leave their nomadic ways and adapted to society. The Gypsies began to settle in various cities throughout Andalusia and found work in the fields of mining, blacksmithing, farming, bread making, shoemaking, bricklaying, fortunetelling, animal training and shearing, as well as dancing, singing, and music.

So it appears that at the end of the 18ᵗʰ century, the music, song, and dance of the Spanish Gypsies began to receive public exposure as they were no longer confined to hidden, private family gatherings strictly within their circle. And here, in the vibrant land of Andalusia, Flamenco was born.

6. FLAMENCO

To fully grasp Flamenco's diverse origins and influences, one must explore Andalusia's sparkling history along with the myriad musical elements found in Flamenco. In this highly debated topic where no theory can ever be fully proven, we must consider the evidence and derive our own conclusions.

Cave paintings in northern Spain dating as far back as 35,000 BCE reveal figures in various dancing poses. Prior to the arrival of the Moors, the Phoenicians brought dances to Spain that are somewhat similar to those still performed today. The Greeks also their left their mark here during the 6th century BCE in the form of artwork illustrating female dancers clapping and playing instruments closely resembling castanets that are used in Spanish folk dances.

Since the 4th century BCE, female singers and dancers from Baética were highly praised, particularly by the Romans, providing a flourishing foundation in southern Spain for the Flamenco that was later to develop.

Cádiz has been famous as a center of song and dance for many centuries. It is believed that during the 4th or 5th century BCE female singers and dancers, who were likely of Phoenician origin, were brought to ancient Rome for entertaining purposes. Mentioned in the writings of Pliny and Strabo, these performers, who used castanets, were known as the *Puellae Gaditanae* — or "Dancing Girls of Cádiz." The dancers, frequently hired to perform at festivals, were legendary for their talent, agility and rich costumes. Their songs or *cantica Gaditanae* became quite popular during Roman times. According to authorities, the lyrics were somewhat provocative, even shocking; the Dancing Girls of Cádiz were considered racy and developed a somewhat lewd reputation. Chronicles tell of a particular favorite named *Telethusa* who danced in Cádiz during the 1st century and was later brought to Rome. Her danced was described as being similar to Eastern dances that also used rhythmic accompaniment. Before she became famous, Telethusa danced at the marketplace with sensuous sways and suggestive gestures as she accompanied herself to the rhythm of her castanet-playing.

The Dancing Girls of Cádiz not only sang but performed palmas and played bronze castanets or finger cymbals with their arms raised high above their heads. Some consider the *Puellae Gaditanas* as the forerunners of Flamenco dancers. Their dance has been described by historians and travelers as sensual, energetic, lively, and fiery. Moves included swirling turns, swaying of the hips, undulations, as well as shaking and quivering as in the oriental shimmy of belly dance. Greek historian and philosopher Strabo (63 BCE–24 AD) wrote about an Egyptian named Eudoxos who lived during the 2nd century BCE; apparently Eudoxos was greatly impressed by the many dancers, singers, musicians, and dancers with *crotalos* (finger cymbals) that he saw in Cádiz. It is this far back that Spain has been celebrated for its dances.

There is no doubt that the origins of Flamenco lie within the integration of local Andalusian folk music and Castilian ballads, with that of the many assorted cultural influences that passed through Andalusia over the centuries. This melting pot includes Phoenician, Greek, North African, and Persian rhythms along with the musical influences of the Orient, Islamic melodies, Gregorian chants, Castilian ballads, liturgical songs of Spain's Jewish community, West African rhythms the slaves brought over, Mozárabic dirges, and lastly, the Moors occupying this land for nearly eight centuries greatly influenced the music of southern Spain — as you can distinctively hear its Arabic influence.

However the most important contributors and the sole interpreters of this vibrant art form were the Gypsies. The Gypsies did not bring Flamenco to Spain, but neither did it exist before their migration. There is nothing similar to Flamenco in any other country which the Gypsies passed through, and nowhere but in Spain is the Gypsy spirit more alive.

However, it is also interesting to observe the Hindi influences and parallels in Flamenco, as similarities can be found in the Northern Indian rhythmic classical dance of Kathak. Kathak originated as a result of the fusion between Hindu and Muslim cultures that occurred during the Muslim conquest of India known as the Mughal Period of the 16th to 19th centuries. One of the greatest cultural achievements during this period of India's history was the construction of the Taj Mahal.

Kathak and Flamenco dance have somewhat similar leg positioning, raised elbows, and rhythmic patterns, along with fast turns and sharp, angular body positions, and arm movements. Graceful movements of the hands are similar as both cultures use splayed finger and curved positions that trace circular motions in the air. The imaginary circles are called *floreos* or "flowerings" of the hand. The arms, hand, and wrist movements of a Flamenco dancer are said to represent a hooded cobra, reminiscent of the Gypsies' distant Hindi origins, where the hands were used to illustrate stories. No stories are told in Flamenco as the hands are merely used for aesthetic purposes to adorn the dance. The hands of a male dancer also trace circles but his fingers are generally kept close together and straight. Female dancers, in particular, perform delicate arm movements that are known as *braceos* (derived from *brazo* or "arm").

Flamenco and Kathak Dancer

Clinard Dance Theatre. Photo by Thierry Emonet.

Flamenco and Kathak both incorporate footwork to the rhythm or counter-rhythm of the music. The Kathak dancer performs percussive footwork with ankle bells while Flamenco dancers use their heels. The intricate and dynamic footwork of Flamenco also has its roots in the complex rhythms of India. This is known as *zapateado* (from *zapato*, the Spanish word for "shoe"(and *tacóneo* is the term used for heelwork (from *tacón* or "heel"), where the sound made is similar to a drumming beat. There are four types of footwork; *golpé* uses the whole foot; *tacón* employs only the heel; *planta* is the striking of the forepart of the foot and *punta* uses only the point of the toe. A combination of these steps is performed to the rhythm or counter-rhythm of the beat. It was during the beginning of the 19th century that percussive footwork was incorporated in the dance.

Flamenco began to take shape during the 15th century when the existing dances and music were modified by the Gypsies who migrated at this time. This art form was secretly cultivated within their private circles. It wasn't until many years later that Gypsies were given the respect and honor they deserve for their development of Flamenco.

By the early 18th century, Flamenco emerged from its isolated existence used only for impromptu private social gatherings among friends and family. Towards the late 18th century the general public began to take notice and Flamenco schools began to emerge. The cradle of Flamenco lies in the cities of Triana in Seville and Jeréz de la Frontera in Cádiz.

Today, there are many different forms or styles of Flamenco music that are known as *palos*, each with its own unique rhythm and structure. There are over 60 palos and some are named after the towns in which they developed; Sevillanas (Seville), Granaínas (Granada), Rondeñas (Ronda), Malagueñas (Málaga), Fandangos de Huelva, and from the eastern coast of the Levante, Murcianas (Murcia) and Cartageneras (Cartagena) are a few.

The first written reference in history to a "Flamenco" or Gypsy party or lifestyle is found in the literature of José Cadalso's *Cartas Marruecas* (Moroccan Letters) dated 1774. During my research, I had often read about this reference, and when I came across a copy of the book at a Flea Market in Cádiz one Sunday morning, I purchased it and immediately turned to Carta VII, which I knew contained this milestone reference. In his collection of letters is a description of a nocturnal Gypsy party: "I will only say that the smoke of cigars, the cries and clapping of Uncle Gregorio, the buzzing of voices, the noise of the castanets, the distressing guitar, the screeching of the Gypsies over the polo (early Flamenco song) so that 'Preciosilla' could dance, the barking of the dogs and the off-key singers, did not let me sleep a wink the entire night." However unflattering, it remains as the first written reference of "Flamenco" or a Gypsy celebration and effectively portrays the environment, overflowing with energy and life.

THE SONG

Flamenco dance and guitar were created from the song. The earliest form of Flamenco consisted of the song or *cante* without any musical instruments for accompaniment, with the exception of a long, dry stick that was held upright and rhythmically tapped on the ground. This is known as *á palo seco*, a term literally translating to "by means of a dry stick." This term also applies to Flamenco that is accompanied solely by rhythmic hand clapping and/or finger snapping.

Some of the most primitive Flamenco songs relate tragic stories of lost love, struggle, desperation, hardship, imprisonment, and death. It was the pain and powerful emotions felt by the Gypsies that created Flamenco.

When listening to the vocals styles of Flamenco, one can clearly detect its Hindu and Arabic influences. The melodic song forms known as *Arabesques* and *Melismas* are fine examples of Arabic influence upon Flamenco. Reminiscent of liturgical chants, Melismas, or extended vocalizations of several notes to a single syllable, are a strong component of Flamenco song. Important characteristics include the extension of vowels, expression of profound feeling, and priority of emotions over lyrics. The *cantaór* (male singer) or *cantaóra* (female singer) must fully surrender to emotions while performing. A *cantante* is used to describe a non-Flamenco singer that performs other styles of song.

Layali is the Arabic term for a vocal improvisation; it is derived from the Arabic word *layla*, meaning "night," and is often sung in Flamenco in the form of *ay, layli, layla, lolailo, lereli, and lerele.*

These Flamenco song fillers may be derived from the similar-sounding Arabic expression *la illaha illa'llah*, translating as "There is no God but Allah." The vocalization of an "ay" often opens a song and can take up to several minutes as sung in varying notes. This is known as *ayeo*, and it allows the singer to warm up and search for the right keys by chanting "*ay, ay, ay*" in various notes and lengths.

One such example is *Cante Jondo*, the oldest form of Flamenco song; cultivated and popularized by the Gypsies it is this one from which most others developed. Cante Jondo or *Cante Hondo* translates as "deep song" or "profound song," for the emotional depths reached by the singer. It is a somber and solemn style that is firmly rooted in Jewish, Arabic, and North African influences combined with Oriental vocal tonalities that are highly evocative of old Moorish melodies as well as the comparable-sounding Muslim call to prayer. Cante Jondo demands great emotional depth from the singer as well as tremendous physical stamina due to its greatly sorrowful and tragic tone. This form emerged from the cries of an oppressed people and was often sung by the Gypsies who were performing monotonous work such as blacksmithing. These blacksmiths released emotional pressure and escaped the drudgery and monotony of their trade by singing to the beat of the hammer, or a *martillo*, striking the iron. The style was called *Martinete* and developed within the metal workers of Triana in Seville. Incarcerated Gypsies also sang from their jails or *carceles* as a form of emotional release. This style, which came to be known as a *Carcelera*, is one of the oldest forms of Cante Jondo and it was born from the misery of imprisoned Gypsies. The Carcelera and Martinete are generally played without guitar accompaniment. Another example of Cante Jondo is the *Soleá*, derived from the word *soleáres*, a shortened version of the Spanish word *soledad* (meaning "solitude" or "loneliness").

Another form of Cante Jondo is the *Peteneras*. Peteneras are a form of Flamenco that is generally slow in rhythm and melancholic in expression; it evolved from the synagogue songs of the Sephardic Jews, as far back as the 15th century. The Petenera comes from a village in Cádiz, near Jeréz de La Frontera, called Paterna de Rivera.

However, a superstitious legend is also behind the origin of this name. It is a tale about a beautiful Jewish courtesan who lived during the 15th century and who broke many men's hearts. The woman was known as La Paternera as she was named after her birth town of Paterna de Rivera. So bewitching was La Paternera that she drove men to madness and even to their deaths:
"La Petenera"

> Si al principio de quererte
> Me hubiera desengañado
> No llegarían las cosas
> Y al terreno que han llegado
>
> Quien te puso Petenera
> No supo ponerte nombre.
> Te debían de que haber puesto

"La perdición de los hombres."

If when I first began loving you
I had not deceived myself,
Things would not have reached
Where they are now.

Whoever named you "Petenera"
Did not know how to name you.
For they should have named you
"The ruin of all men."

The mystique surrounding Peteneras is that some Gypsies refuse to perform this style as they believe it will bring bad luck, since the legend is connected with such death and sorrow. Petenera herself supposedly died a tragic and violent death at the hand of a scorned lover. This song form has also been considered to belong to the next group, although I believe that Peteneras lean more toward Cante Jondo.

Cante Intermedio is less tragic or profound and is often more Oriental in feel than Cante Jondo. Included in this group are *Malagueñas, Granaínas, Tarantos, Tientas* as well as *Mineras* that were sung by the Gypsies who worked in the mines, or *minas.* Cante Intermedio often contains influences and elements of Latin American music, such as the *Rumba Gitana, Tango Gitanos, Milongas, Guajiras,* and *Columbianas.* Many serious enthusiasts, however, do not consider these as Flamenco, aside from the fact that they are sung in Flamenco-style.

As progress is inevitable, a faster, happier, lighter, shorter, more frivolous form known as *Cante Chico* or "little song" also developed. Cante Chico is upbeat and more suited to dancing while the lyrics convey feelings of happiness, hope, pride, humor, and love. There are many forms of Cante Chico including *Alegrías*, meaning "joy," and the lively and fast *Bulerías*, from the word *burla*, meaning "mockery" or "joke," that originated in Jeréz de la Frontera. When a song is interpreted by a particular palo, such as bulerías, it is called *por bulerías*, meaning "by bulerías." Bulerías and Alegrías are the most popular forms of Flamenco dance today.

Camarón de la Isla (1950-1992), born in Cádiz, is the most celebrated cantaór of all time. He was born José Monje Cruz and received the nickname "The Shrimp" (El Camarón) from his uncle when he was a young, thin, fair, and light-haired boy. Despite this, Camarón possessed exceptional tuning capacity and expressed gut-wrenching emotions through his vocals that led him to become the model that all future cantaórs would follow to this day.

Some of today's most popular cantaórs include Enrique Morente from Granada, Agujetas from Cádiz, and Fosforito from Córdoba. Among the most popular current cantaóras are Carmen Linares from Jaén, Estrella Morente from Granada, and Niña Pastori from Cádiz.

A young and talented Gypsy singer and one of my personal favorites is Sonia Priego, from Seville, better known as *La Húngara*. Her manager informed me that she is one of the artists that sell the most albums throughout Spain and that she had completed a very successful tour of over sixty concerts throughout the country in 2005. In her moving 2003 hit song "*A Camarón*" , she pays homage to Camarón; it was written and composed by her manager, Francisco Carmona.

> Y el mejor de to los tiempos fuiste tú El Camarón
> Embajador del Flamenco, voz de oro hecha pasión
> De tu garganta salieron quejíos de un corazón
> Al compás de bulerías que el mundo entero las aplaudió.
>
> Camarón, Camarón
> Tu eres lo mas grande que el Flamenco dio
> Camarón, Camarón
> Para ti mi canto, fuiste el mejor.
>
> Como el agua clara, pura y transparente
> Eran los metales de tu voz ardiente
> De llorar El Tomate y Paco de Lucia
> De llorar los tangos y la bulerías
> Desde que te fuiste ya no hay alegría...
>
> And the greatest of all time was you, El Camarón
> Ambassador of Flamenco with a golden voice of passion
> From your throat emerged cries from the heart
> To the rhythm of *bulerías* that the whole world applauded.
>
> Camarón, Camarón
> You are greatest gift that Flamenco ever gave us
> Camarón, Camarón
> For you, my song, you were the best.
>
> Like clear water, pure and transparent
> Was the timbre of you ardent voice
> Crying *El Tomate* and *Paco De Lucía*

Crying the tangos and the *bulería*
Since you went away, there is no more joy.

THE DANCE

Compared to other dance forms, Flamenco is fairly young in age, being roughly two centuries old. It was only towards the end of the 19th century that it became commercially popular, when non-Gypsies or Payos began to learn the art form. Flamenco dance ultimately spread through the remaining provinces of Andalusia, each contributing its own personal inspiration and style.

"Gypsies" by Manuel Ruiz, 1960

The dance falls in the three same categories; *baile grande, baile intermedio,* and the faster, more lively, *baile chico,* all with their corresponding music. The male dancer is known as a *bailaór* and a female dancer is a *bailaóra.* A *bailarín* or *bailarína* is a classically-trained dancer and can be used to describe a Flamenco dancer who is classically trained but this is not always intended as a compliment. A *bailarín* is the equivalent in dance to what a *cantante* is in song; that is, a dancer or singer not performing Flamenco.

Male dancers exhibit traits of defiance, pride, strength, and confidence. Female dancers also display these qualities but they incorporate femininity, grace, and often a sense of playfulness and fun, as well. In a sense, Flamenco dance is the antithesis of ballet. Ballet is performed with the feet pointing off the ground with the body reaching upwards in a light and airy manner. In Flamenco, the eyes are often downcast and the feet are driven hard into the floor, rendering the dance heavier and more grounded. Carolina Varga Dinicu, of Rom origin (better known as *Morocco*) is a Flamenco and Oriental dance instructor and historian. She is also a leading authority on the history of dances and she states that the foot and leg movements of ballet are actually derived from the Basque men's folk dance of Spain.

Today's most popular bailaóres include Joaquín Cortés from Córdoba, Antonio Canales from Seville, and Rafael Amargo from Granada. Bailaóras include Sara Baras from Cádiz, Maria Pages from Seville, and born outside of Andalusia and Spain, La Tati from Madrid, and Eva Yerbabuena from Frankfurt.

The tight-fitting dress of the Flamenco dancer is reminiscent of the attractive shape of the guitar. Its origins lie within the Andalusian women of the mid 19th century who began wearing these colorful, often dotted, dresses at the annual *Feria de Abril* or April Fair. By the 1920s the dress had been adopted and accepted into the world of Flamenco. The dancer would often embellish the dress with a fringed shawl and may wear a bright flower in her hair or a high ornamental comb made from tortoise shell known as a *peineta* (from *peine* meaning "comb") that not only adorns but holds the tight bun in place. Her props could include a colorful fan or *abanico* that would open, close, and flicker according to the choreography and the dancer's moods. In more modest times, the fan was used as an extension of the hand and had its own language that allowed the woman to communicate her emotional feelings. Some of these included touching her right cheek with the fan, meaning "yes," while the left meant the opposite. Placing the handle to her lips meant "kiss me" and fanning very slowly communicated that she was married. Reference to the first use of the Spanish fan goes back to the 14th century and it has since been an important component of Spanish culture.

A large triangular fringed shawl known as a *Mantón de Manila* is also used to accentuate the dance; it is twirled or tossed around, somewhat similar to the way the veil is used in Oriental dance. It also can be manipulated within the choreography to simulate the graceful moves of the matador's cape. The origins of the shawl go back to ancient China; shawls have been popular in Spain since the *Conquistadores* first brought them back from expeditions into the Philippines in their galleons laden with exotic goods, beginning in the 16th century.

The men, on the other hand, wear slimming, dark slacks with fancy shirts and waist-length tight jackets. The Córdoban hat is another important symbol of Andalusian culture. Traditionally worn by the man, it can nowadays also be found adorning the head of a woman. The hat was worn not only by dancers but by matadors, Andalusian horse riders, and by people participating in religious festivals or fairs known as *romerías*. With its birthplace in Córdoba, the use of this felt hat with a wide and flat brim became quite popular during the 19th century. Nowadays they are available in many shades; however, black remains the traditional color.

Flamenco is generally improvised as it comes from the soul and is danced from within. The term *gracia* is a special compliment to a Flamenco dancer. No one word alone is synonymous in English. The best equivalent might be a combination of interpretations: spark, wit, charm, fun, as well as being cheeky, flirtatious, confident, amusing, and slightly humorous all at once. One cannot *be* "gracia" but must *have* "gracia."

This is not to be confused with *duende,* another difficult concept to translate. It is like magic; a trance-like state or the temporary possession of an overwhelming feeling sometimes referred to as a demon or spirit that inhabits the body and soul of one overcome with emotion while enjoying or performing Flamenco song, dance, or guitar. When *duende* enters the artist, it brings intense inspiration or extreme sorrow in expression, therefore greatly improving the performance. Not every artist can "possess" duende, only the truly gifted. *Duende* can also temporarily possess the soul of one who is truly affected by another's moving performance.

"Carmen Amaya" by Manuel Ruiz, 2006

CARMEN AMAYA

Without a doubt, the best Flamenco dancer of all time is Carmen Amaya (1913-1963). What Camarón was to Flamenco song, she was to Flamenco dance. Born in Barcelona and of Gypsy heritage, Carmen began performing at the age of four, accompanied by her musician father, *El Chino,* who played guitar in the taverns of Barcelona. Her mother Micaela Amaya was also a dancer, as was her aunt Juana Amaya, who performed under the name of *La Faraóna.*

Carmen was a full-blooded Gypsy who descended from the "Chavori e Baraje" tribe that traces its origins back to India. Although her ancestors were from Sacromonte, Granada, she was born in the Gypsy quarter of Somorrostro in Barcelona. She often dressed as a bailaór, wearing masculine pants and a vest when performing; although she was not the first, it did become one of her trademarks.

Carmen was a small woman, barely 5 feet tall, but she performed with the furor and frenzy of a giant, unlike any other throughout Flamenco's history.

She introduced the world to Flamenco dance through her international tours that were often accompanied by guitar virtuoso Sabicas. Carmen Amaya essentially combined the masculine strength and aggression of a male dancer with the grace and exotic elegance of a female dancer. Her Scorpio gaze pierced right through you as she took you under her spell with her mesmerizing *zapateado* that traditionally had been exclusively danced by men. In the past, female dancers seldom performed footwork and focused primarily on graceful hands, arms, upper body, and swaying hips.

Arabic Lute

Carmen's great-niece, Omayra Amaya, has also followed her footsteps and continued the Amaya Flamenco Dance Company & School tradition currently based in Miami, Florida. Omayra speaks of her great aunt in her documentary titled "Gypsy Heart," describing how she revolutionized Flamenco dance through her electrifying footwork. "She was the best dancer in the world. I grew up hearing about her and hearing how good she was. She's been a great inspiration to me in the sense that she believed in something and she went about it, she was capable of doing, and she struggled and went against traditional Flamenco of the time, and later she became recognized."

The Guitar

The Spanish guitar is a descendant of the Greco/Assyrian *kithára* or lyre. The lyre itself is predated by the lute of ancient Egypt, as seen on bas-reliefs dated 3700 BCE. This musical instrument was known as the *Cithara* by the Romans who introduced it to southern Spain when this region became part of the Roman Empire. This flat-backed instrument evolved into the *Guitarra Latina* or the Spanish Guitar.

While the Arabs knew it as *al-Qitara*, they introduced their own stringed musical instrument to the peninsula in the form of *al-ud* (or *laud*, in Castilian). This Arabic lute of Mesopotamian origin was most likely introduced to Andalusia by Ziryab during the 9th century. The oud or lute has a rounded back and came to be known as the *guitarra Morisca.* It was the preferred musical instrument in the Arab world, yet was unknown to Greece and Rome.

As far back as the 11th century, high quality lutes were being crafted in Seville; however this musical instrument was banned after the Reconquest as it served as a reminder of centuries of Moorish oppression to the Christians. During the 16th century it was replaced by the *vihuela*, that displayed features of the guitarra Latina and the guitarra Morisca. The vihuela was quite popular during the 15th and 16th centuries, particularly within the royal courts of Spain.

The guitar, as an accompaniment to song, is first mentioned in *La Explicacíon del Guitarra* published in 1773. As an instrument playing a secondary role in Flamenco, the guitar eventually reached equal heights of importance as song and dance. The guitarists, who complemented the singers and dancers, began to gain attention and by the mid 19th century guitar became the primary musical accompanying instrument of Flamenco song; guitar solos eventually developed.

Federico García Lorca is Spain's most beloved modern poet. He was born in Granada in 1898 and was killed in Granada by firing squad during the Civil War by the Nationalists in 1936. García Lorca dedicated a poem to the guitar:

"Las Seis Cuerdas"

La guitarra,
hace llorar a los suenos.
El sollozo de las almas

perdidas,
se escapa por su boca
redonda.
Y como la tarantula
teje una gran estrella
para cazar suspiros,
que flotan en su negro
aljibe de madera.

"The Six Strings"

The guitar
makes dreams weep.
The sobbing of lost souls
escapes from its round mouth.
And like the tarantula
it weaves a giant star
to capture sighs
that float in its black
cistern of wood.

*"Palmas" by
Manuel Ruiz, 1960*

Before the guitar was used for accompaniment, other methods of maintaining the beat have persisted over the centuries and remain an integral part of Flamenco today. The rhythm or *compás* is maintained by *palmas* or rhythmic and counter rhythmic hand clapping, performed by *palmeros*.

Palmas is an art in itself. When the hands are cupped as they strike each other, the sound is muffled, hollow, or soft; these are called *palmas sordas* (deaf or muted). This sound is generally used for accompaniment as well as for opening a song by the cantaór or cantaóra. When the fingers strike the palm of the other hand, it is called *palmas secas* (dry, or sharp) and is generally used to increase excitement at peak moments. When in syncopation, one group of palmeros may repeatedly perform *tak* while the other inserts *ka* in between at half time resulting in *tak-ka, tak-ka, ta-ka*.... Great comprehension and skill of compás is required to be a palmero.

Jaleadóres also animate and provide encouragement to the performance by spontaneously praising, shouting, and calling out to the dancer, singer, or guitarist at the appropriate times. The jaleadóres are usually palmeros and they sit or stand behind the performers. The audience also plays an important role in the encouragement of the artist. Common expressions or vocal outbursts from the audience or jaleadóres include "*¡ále!*," "*¡olé!*," "*¡eso es!*" (that's it!), "*toma toma!*" (take that!) and *¡vamo ya!* (let's go!) It is important to mention that timing is everything, when verbally encouraging the artist; it cannot be done at just any moment.

Other methods include rhythmic *pitos* or finger snaps and rapping of the knuckles called *nudillos* (deriving from *nudos* or knuckles) on wooden surface such as a table top. When Carmen Amaya was ill, towards the end of her life, she often performed nudillos with the same furor as when she danced.

A large wooden box known as a *cajón* (from *caja* or "box") is also used as a percussion instrument that is played between the knees as one sits upon it.

The use of castanets is traditional in such regional Andalusian dances as *Sevillanas, Fandangos de Huelva, Fandanguillos,* and *Tanguillos de Cádiz* but is not traditional to authentic Flamenco. The Gypsies disliked playing castanets and preferred marking the rhythm with pitos, synchronized palmas, and clicking of the tongue. The reason that castanets are not used in true Flamenco is that the delicate hand and finger movements of the dancer, reminiscent to their Hindi heritage, is greatly limited or impeded while playing the castanets and so they are a part of local folk dances exclusively. Graceful hand, wrist, and arm movements are an indispensable component of authentic Flamenco and castanets are incompatible with this key element.

Dancing with castanets is believed to be of Phoenician origin and their use eventually spread throughout the Mediterranean world. However, it was in Spain where castanets were preserved and perfected becoming traditional to local folk dances as well as an integral component in the country's cultural heritage. During the 11th and 12th centuries, the castanets were attached to the middle fingers as some dancers still play in folk dances. It wasn't until the 18th century that they began being attached to the thumbs as generally played today.

It is generally accepted that castanets were introduced to Spain during the late 19th century by ballet dancers who also performed Flamenco.

This percussion instrument can be played by marking the rhythm with single strokes called *golpes* (meaning "hits") and rolling the fingers, or trilling, called *carretillas* (meaning "wheelbarrow") for a speedy rattling effect. Both sets come in a slightly different pitch; the higher- sounding pair called *hembra* (female) is worn on the right and the lower-tone pair called *macho* (male) is held in the left hand. It is usually the right hand that performs the carretilla while the left hand marks the beat with golpes.

The Spanish word *castañuelas* is derived from the diminutive form of *castaña*, meaning "chestnut" which they resemble in shape. The Gitanos of Andalusia call them *palillos*, meaning "little sticks." Using small sticks as musical accompaniment goes as far back as the days of ancient Egypt. Today, few Gypsies play castanets.

During the 20th century, the guitar graduated to a respected solo form completing the trinity of Flamenco: *el cante*, (the song), *el toque* (referring to the guitar and translating as "the touch" but used in Castilian as a synonym for "play" as in "playing the guitar") and *el baile* (the dance), each evolving into an art form in itself. The real magic begins when an impromptu artistic dialogue is formed between the guitarist, dancer, and singer.

The traditional way of holding a guitar is in its vertical position. Paco de Lucía from Algeciras, Cádiz (b. 1947), still plays in this manner. My personal favorite guitar pieces of Paco de Lucía are "Ziryab" and "Almoraíma," for their heavy Oriental feel, and "Granada" for the memories it evokes. El Lebrijano, born Juan Fernández Peña in Lebrija, Seville, in 1941, is another renowned singer who has also done brilliant solo work and has collaborated with Paco de Lucía and the *Orquesta Andalusi de Tanger*. Another popular guitarist that performed with Paco de Lucia is *Tomatito* or *El Tomate* from Almería. Born José Fernández Torres in 1958, Tomatito was virtually unknown until he was discovered by Camarón and he remained his best friend until his untimely death. Tomatito's three daughters formed a pop group known as *Las Ketchup* and they recorded the worldwide summer hit "The Ketchup Song," also known as *"Aserejé,"* that was released in 2002. These young girls are locally known as "Las Córdobesas mas famosas del mundo" ("The world's most famous Córdoban women").

Although Gypsy Flamenco is exclusive to Spain, a very popular group of Gitanos from southern France known as the *Gipsy Kings* introduced their Rumba Flamenca to the world during the late eighties. With Gypsy ancestry from the Catalonian region of Spain, the Gipsy Kings deserve much credit for the recently renewed interest in Spanish music. Although it is not traditional Flamenco, their wonderful sound can best be described as fusion pop-oriented Spanish Gypsy music. Famous around the globe, the Gipsy Kings remain less appreciated in Spain, where they are criticized for their so-called mass commercialism.

Some of the greatest Flamenco guitarists of all time include Ramón Montoya (1880-1949), from Madrid, who is known as the founder of modern-style solo Flamenco guitar; Sabicas (born Augustín Castellón Campos) from Pamplona (1912-1990); and Andrés Segovia of Jaén (1893 -1987). Over the years, classical Flamenco as performed by these masters became a separate entity from Gypsy Flamenco, the latter being less refined or sophisticated than its classical form.

THE GOLDEN AGE OF FLAMENCO

During the late 18th to early 19th century, the demand for public Flamenco performances was on the rise. Gypsy dancers and musicians were hired by the wealthy and the elite to perform at parties or *juergas* as well as to entertain in courtyards, taverns, and festivals.

The stage was set for Flamenco venues to arise. During the mid 19th century, *Café Cantantes* (singing cafés) began appearing, exposing the art beyond its natural and private Gypsy habitat to the general Payo or non-Gypsy public. These popular settings were a cross between a tavern and a theater; they managed to breathe new life once again into Flamenco, which rapidly became quite popular and fashionable. Alcohol was served and Flamenco was performed by small ensembles of singers, dancers, and guitarists known as a *cuadro Flamenco*. The first Café Cantante opened in Seville in the year 1842. This is the actual moment that defined the beginning of Flamenco as the professional art form that we know and respect today.

By 1860 the cafés began to attract more and more attention and many began to surface in other major Andalusian towns as well as throughout the country. These cafés were visited by all classes of Spaniards and foreign visitors; Flamenco was no longer exclusive to the Gypsies. Through this art form, everyone came together in the name of music, song, and dance. The best performances were given at this time and it became known as *La Edad de Oro del Flamenco*, "The Golden Age of Flamenco."

Although Flamenco soared to popular heights in these cafés, they eventually began to be criticized for the loss of authenticity. Performances became commercialized and began incorporating Andalusí musical elements, such as castanets, in order to attract a wider audience. At this time, Payos also began to learn the art, which managed in the process to forfeit some of its most primitive — and authentic —elements. By the late 19th century, although Flamenco had reached a wider audience, it had sacrificed some of its purity in the development.

After the Café Cantantes came the popular *tablaos* that have been presenting Flamenco shows mainly for tourists since the early 1950s. The name of these shows and venues is derived from *tabla*, meaning "plank," or "board," in reference to the raised platform that was built as a stage for the performers. Inspired by the Café Cantantes, this new, bigger, and better version once again presented authentic and traditional Flamenco. Tablaos met with a highly enthusiastic response. The first of its kind opened in Madrid in 1954 and focused on presenting the purest form of Flamenco available. Despite the inevitable increasing local competition, it continued to be successful until the death of the owner in 1975; it was permanently closed. It was named after the Gypsy festivities exclusive to the Sacromonte Caves of Granada, the prestigious *Tablao La Zambra*.

7. Zambra

The Arabic word *Zambra* has several meanings but it originally meant the noises made by certain musical instruments and lively crowds. It also signified a loud and animated party or celebration that was usually held outdoors, or a festival. These boisterous and bustling festivities generally lasted until dawn; many diversions such as animated conversation, poetry reading, story-telling, joke-sharing, as well as music, song, and dance, took place.

During the 15th century, *Don Pedro de Cardona*, Count of Golisano and Ambassador to King Alfonso V of Aragón, provided a description of the Moors as a people fond of tales and jokes, devoted to dance, leisure time, songs, and especially any pastime of a noisy and boisterous nature.

Historical documents indicate that the popular music of the Moriscos between the 16th and 18th centuries were the *Zambras* and *Leilas*. The Zambras of al-Andalus were passed down to the Moriscos who kept the tradition alive. The Zambra, according to Sebastian de Covarrubias' *Tesoro de la Lengua Castellana*, dated 1611, is "Moorish dance; music with wind instruments of the sounds of pipes and flutes." According to Matteo's *Language of Spanish Dance*, Zambras were popular in Seville after the fall of Cordoba during the 13th century, where artists among Moors, Christians, and Jews were sought. However, this is the only reference to Moorish Zambras outside of Granada that I have come across. Matteo also describes a few Zambra dance steps such as the *Paseo de Zambra* (Zambra travel) and the *Vuelta de Zambra* (Zambra turn.)

We can safely say that the Zambras were created and popularized by the Moriscos of Spain as they drew on the Andalusian and Moorish influences already present. The Moorish Zambras are exclusive to southern Spain; they are not found in any other Arabic country. No historical record has been found detailing how the Zambra of the Moriscos was danced. However, according to *Ginés Pérez de Hita*, one night during the 16th century, at a particular Zambra at the home of *Zayda*, "they danced the Zambra, all holding hands with each other as was the custom with that particular dance."

In John A. Crow's *Spain, the Root and the Flower*, he lists the common musical instruments in al-Andalus during the 13th century as the lute, fiddle, trumpet, harp, bagpipe, castanets, flute, pipes, and drums. He adds that the music was mainly based on the popular folk tunes of that era.

After the Reconquest, the celebrations of the Moriscos of Granada became known as Zambras; there they joyfully danced to the music of bagpipes and kettledrums. These Zambras were deeply rooted in the nearly eight hundred years of Moorish influence. Zambra also referred to the group of musicians and any festival where dancing and singing was accompanied by palmas and such instruments as the *mizhar* (lute), vihuela, *rababa* (Arabic fiddle), *kemanjah* (violin), *pandereta* (tambourine), *tar* (small tambourine), *darbouka* (Arabic clay drum), *atabal* (base drum), *sunuy* (finger cymbals or *sany* in singular form), and from the flute family, *zomalí*, *xabeba*, *qassaba*, as well as bracelets and anklets with little jingling bells or cymbals (known as *jalajil*) that the dancers wore. Often, small high-pitched brass finger cymbals known in Spanish as *chinchines* (for the sound they emitted) or *platillos* (meaning "little disks" that they resembled) were used to accompany the dance. The tradition of palmas and encouraging a performer by shouting words of praise (such as *olé*, from the Arabic expression *wa'Allah* ,meaning "by God!") in Flamenco goes back to the Zambras of the Moriscos.

By the 15th century the dance of the Moriscos spread throughout Europe and particularly to Great Britain where many believe it evolved into the *Morris Dance*. In 1524 the first evidence of the Arabic word "Zambra" appeared in reference to the religious celebrations of the Christians. The document stated that the Moors were requested, hired and paid eight royal coins or *reales* to perform and bring their Zambras to the Christian festivals. Between the 12th and 15th centuries, Arab and Jewish musicians from the south were being recruited for the Christian courts of northern Spain and by the 16th century, these musicians known as *zambreros* and *juglares* were frequently hired to perform.

During the 16th century, Spanish folk music continued to merge with Arabic sounds and styles as the *Zambra, Fandango, Zorongo, Chacona* and the *Zarabanda* (meaning "noise" in Arabic), that was danced with castanets and tambourines. The Chacona and Zarabanda were performed towards the end of the 16th century and the Zorongo and Fandango are believed to have developed in Spain during the 17th or 18th century. The Fandango is therefore older than Flamenco; it is considered an Andalusian folk dance of Moorish origin that spread throughout Spain. It has remained popular ever since. However, during the 18th century, the Catholic Church banned the dance as it was considered improper, vulgar, and immoral.

Also from the Fandango family are the *Fandangos Grande* (Big Fandangos) and *Fandanguillos* (Little Fandangos). Moroccan artist Hakim wrote and sang an intense and powerful version of the Fandango, sung in Arabic, accompanied by a Flamenco guitar. The track is called *Fandango Darabia* and it is a superb example of how the two cultures produce exquisite music when integrated with each other.

The clothing during this century of Moorish musicians is illustrated and described in Christoph Weiditz's (c. 1500-1559) *Das Trachtenbuch des Christoph Weiditz von seinen Reisen nach Spanien (1529) und Niederlanden (1531/32)*. "The Morisco musicians wear sandals and mimic the sound of castanets with their fingers as they dance with each other. One tambourine player wears a green cap with red trimming, a green jacket richly adorned in silver, a blue and red belt and a pocket decorated in gold with two golden buttons. The violinist wears a dark violet cap, a jacket in a rich red hue adorned in gold and his violin is brownish-yellow. The third musician wears a blue coat decorated in silver, with sleeves adorned with gold trim."

Another account states that during the early 17th century, the *Morisca* was danced to the sounds of the lute. In one particular show, three or four dancing Moors and six women appeared dressed in silk suits with large, wide sleeves of colored silk slit at the sides, small hats and lined shoes, wearing silver and gold rings, bracelets, necklaces, and "monstrously large" earrings. The dancers marked the rhythm with finger snaps and castanets made from ivory or wood.

After the Christian conquest and up to the 18th century, Moorish music and dance of the Moriscos continued to flourish in southern Spain, finding its way into liturgical celebrations. However, certain conditions were implemented in its use as the faith of the Christians had to be honored rather than that of the Muslims. Absolutely no mention was to be made to Muhammad during these festivities; this was not to be a Moorish celebration but a Christian festival with hired Morisco musicians, singers, dancers, and other performers.

Queen Isabel of Portugal, wife of King Carlos I of Spain, was an ardent defender of the music and Zambras of the Moriscos that was banned by the Archbishop of Granada. Her Majesty inquired as to why such a ban was imposed and demanded an explanation. On the 20th of June in the year 1530 she wrote the Archbishop a lengthy letter on this matter, recalling that in 1526 a ban was ordered against the ceremonies of the Moriscos or Zambras that had caused much sorrow to the Moriscos or converted Christians. The Moriscos insisted that the Zambras did not in any way insult or betray Christianity nor did they implement or promote any Muslim belief or ceremony whatsoever and should not have been prohibited. In summary the Queen interceded on behalf of the Moriscos stating that Zambras without Moorish ceremonies or any insults to the Catholic faith, and no dishonesty of any kind, should in fact be permitted.

However, King Felipe II soon instated various laws that promoted the hatred of Moriscos and all that was their culture, such as the prohibition of the Arabic language, traditional customs, and manner of dress. Also banned was the use of Moorish musical instruments and song. In a document written in 1566 by General Diego de Espinosa referring to the inquisition that was run in collaboration with King Felipe II, certain conditions are stipulated: "All rites, festivals, ceremonies and wedding celebrations of the Moors are prohibited. All must comply with the appreciation and ways of the Santa Madre Iglesia and in the form that the faithful Christians had done before; and during days of a marriage ceremony, the doors of the houses are to remain open, and the same on Friday afternoons and all the days of festivals; and that there will be no zambras nor leilas with Moorish musical instruments or songs of any form, even though through them, nothing is said or sung in these zambras against the Christian religion."

Under the Edict of the Accusations of the Santa Inquisición ("Holy Inquisition"), it was prohibited to marry according to the rites or customs of the Moors or to sing Moorish songs or give Zambras or Leilas performed with forbidden Arabic musical instruments. It is within these Zambras that the origins of Flamenco lie simmering.

Cueva de Los Amayas in Sacromonte

At this time in history, the Moriscos began to blend with and hide among the Gypsies in order to remain in the country. The Zambras of the Moriscos persisted and eventually were integrated with the popular Zambras of the Spanish Gypsies known as *Zambra Gitana*. Towards the second half of the 19th century, the word "Zambra" reappears in Granada after several hundreds years of absence, with reference to the Gypsy celebrations of dance, music and palmas. The Zambra Mora (Moorish Party) had been replaced by the Zambra Gitanas, exclusive to the Gypsies of Sacromonte. These new Zambras were comprised of a group or family of Gypsies led by a captain that presented commercial song and dance to the paying public. This leader was responsible for naming the group as well as directing, arranging and choreographing the shows. The Zambras were composed of one or two guitarists and singers with at least 4 to 6 male and female dancers.

The first Zambra that we know about was organized during the second half of the 19th century in the Sacromonte in Granada. The event was hosted by Antonio Torcuato Martin, of Gypsy blood, who went by the name of *El Cujón*, a variation of his original off-colored nickname that Spanish-speaking readers will immediately recognize. Martin was a gifted singer and guitarist who presented Zambras in a decorated room of his blacksmith shop with the best dancers, singers, and musicians he could find, including *La Golondrina* and *María La Canastera*. The cave of *Los Amayas* is also worth mentioning as it is dated to the late 1800s and belonged to Juan Amaya and his family.

The Amayas are a true-blooded Gypsy family of Flamenco entertainers that for generations have been performing Zambras. The sign by the door proudly reads, *Cueva de los Amayas, fundadores de las Zambras en el Sacromonte* (Cave of the Amayas, founders of the first Zambras in the Sacromonte).

The word "Zambra" has also been used to describe a trilogy of traditional Andalusian Gypsy ceremonial or prenuptial songs born in the Sacromonte that have been performed at weddings since the middle of the 19th century. This Zambra style falls under the *cante chico* or *baile chico* category, being joyful and light in nature. This very antiquated and lively folk dance and music is composed of three parts: *La Alboreá* (or *Alboleá*), *La Cachucha*, and *La Mosca*, each representing the different stages or special moments of a Gypsy wedding. The Alboreá (contracted version of *alboreada*, meaning "dawning") is considered the true nuptial song and dance of the Gypsies of Granada and is the first to be performed after the bride's handkerchief has proven the legitimacy of her virtue. La Cachucha is the first ritual dance performed by the couple surrounded by their family and friends. The song of the Cachucha is believed to have originated in Cádiz during the early 1800s. La Mosca or "The Fly" closes the ceremonial Zambra that represents the Gypsy wedding.

The wedding theme is often incorporated with costumes into the Zambras of the Sacromonte. In these shows you will also see and hear the Gypsies perform to the lively Bulerías, Rumbas, Alegrías, Tango Gitanos, Seguiríyas, Martinetes, Fandangos, and Zambra styles. The latter is slower in tempo and Arabic in feel; all that the Gypsies inherited or borrowed from the Moors is evident in the Zambra. Granada is considered as the Land of Fandangos of which there would be no memory of this style had the Gypsies of Sacromonte not incorporated them into their Zambras.

The Zambras of the Sacromonte have often been criticized for their rough or amateur performances; however, many aficionados prefer the authenticity and excitement over more highly staged and controlled performances.

Cueva de Maria la Canastera in Sacromonte, Granada

One year in Granada I interviewed Enrique "El Canastero" Carmona Cortéz, son of Maria La Canastera. When I asked him what Zambra meant, he explained, "Zambra is the folkloric Alboreá, La Cachucha, and La Mosca. Those who offer Zambras in the area and do not incorporate these three song and dances are merely tablaos," as he waved his hand in the air in dismissal. "In the cave of Maria La Canastera," he continued, "they are still being performed in every show. Ours is the only true and authentic Zambra that incorporate the three ritual dances." When I asked him about his mother, he began, "My mother died 39 years ago. She first danced at the cave of La Coja and the Amayas even before El Cujon's. She opened this very Zambra in 1953 and her nieces, nephews, and grandchildren maintain her tradition by performing here almost every night for tourists. My mother was friends with Carmen Amaya, did you see the poster?" as he pointed to it on the wall. "She was in one of her movies, dancing in Sacromonte in "Maria de la O."

Maria La Canastera in center and Carmen Amaya at right, in 1929, both 16 years of age

ZAMBRA MORA

When the Gypsies arrived, they easily identified with the Oriental dance style of the Spanish Moors, incorporating some of their music and dance forms that could have been Flamenco in its early stages and not yet fully defined. The Gypsies not only borrowed the term "Zambra" from the Moors by incorporated it into their Zambra Gitana, but played the *Zambra Por Moro* with a pulsating, earthy rhythm somewhat similar to that of the *Tangos* and *Tarantos*. Of all the forms of Flamenco, it is the Zambra Mora that has the strongest Arabic feel. It is not to be confused with the medieval-sounding *Zambra Granadina*, composed by Isaac Albeníz and Andrés Segovia.

Quite often, the concept of Zambra and Zambra Mora are confused. Although both are of Moorish origin, they are two separate entities. To summarize, the Zambra is a pure Gypsy Flamenco song, music, dance performance and celebration held in the caves of the Sacromonte, composed of artists usually from the same family. Zambra was not only the name of the festivity but the locale where it was held. This is strictly Gypsy Flamenco and bears no resemblance whatsoever or relation to the distinct rhythm and Oriental tonalities of the Zambra Mora style of Flamenco song or guitar.

Zambra Mora is a rhythmic arrangement found in the music of Flamenco made popular by guitarist Sabicas and named in honor of the Zambras or celebrations of the Moors for the strong Arabic flavor. It is slightly different than the more Arabic-sounding *Danza Mora*, *Danza Arabe* and *Arabescas*, yet all ultimately fall under the category of Flamenco. Zambra Mora is a form of song and guitar but not a dance form.

Carmen Amaya has often been described as dancing a Zambra. Amaya did not dance a Zambra but danced Flamenco *at* a Zambra. Here is where the confusion arises; it is not the name of a Spanish dance. Furthermore, and recently, Zambra Mora has been described as a dance that integrates Flamenco with Oriental dance. Nowhere have I been able to confirm this throughout my years of research in southern Spain. What is being described is actually modern Spanish/Arabic fusion dance or Oriental Flamenco, as Zambra Mora was never a specific dance form in itself but was a musical form of the Mozárabic Zambra, named after the Moorish celebrations.

Guitar Shop on Cuesta de Gomérez, Granada

During my research when I have inquired about Zambra Mora, Flamenco performers and aficionados always responded with a raised eyebrow followed by slight dismissal, as if to say, "that is not true Flamenco." Nowhere is this more evident than in a discussion I had with a Flamenco guitarist during a visit to Granada; this finally confirmed any remaining doubts.

As I was making my way up to the Alhambra one September afternoon, walking up the *Cuesta de Gomérez*, I was immediately captivated by the sound of Flamenco guitar playing nearby. Noticing it came from small shop that repaired guitars across the street, I decided to venture in. Inside was a customer brilliantly playing the guitar that I had heard from across the street. I introduced myself to the man behind the counter and he informed me that he was Francisco (Paco) Manuel Díaz, owner of the shop.

Venta de Gallo in Sacromonte, Granada

We began chatting and he told me that he was a tocaór and has been playing guitar at Zambras in the Sacromonte for over three decades. Sensing my interest, he inserted a tape into his VCR and showed me video footage from the early 70s of him playing guitar with Juan Heredia at a Zambra Gitana in the Sacromonte. (Heredia is the owner of the very popular Flamenco venue "*Venta El Gallo*" in Sacromonte.)

In one scene from the video, Paco and Juan were accompanied by several mature women wearing ordinary housedresses singing and dancing to their hearts' content, to the rhythm of the guitars, as they danced with their heads held high and arms raised above.

At these Zambras, Paco began to explain, the "abuelitas" (little grandmothers) would improvise and "colorfully" change the lyrics to the great amusement of all. "Oh, the things they would say!" he fondly remembered, nodding his head laughing. It was clear that he missed those days. He pointed out each person in the video as if he was introducing them to me in person and solemnly said, "But most of them are not with us anymore."

I remember having read that Zambra Mora may have been danced in Sacromonte and decided to question him about it. He remained silent, slowly turned around and picked up his guitar from behind the counter and began playing this dramatic and mystifying rhythm. He then looked at me and stated, "There is no such thing." Once a Spaniard makes a statement like that, there is no arguing. "That is something Moorish, not Spanish," he continued. "It came the Moors who remained. That is not true Flamenco; it is just music, a type of music. Sabicas invented it and it is fantasy."

When I visited the Centro Andaluz de Flamenco in Jeréz del la Frontera, I was impressed with its art exhibits, museum, archives, lithographs, video, and book library. It also contains a small theater showing hourly visual presentations on Flamenco. Founded in 1958, this organization is dedicated to the promotion of the study and preservation of Flamenco in its purest form. It is housed in the late 18th century Palacio de Pemartín in Plaza San Juan.

I decided to propose the same question to the young but very knowledgeable librarian. She smiled and explained, "This subject is quite controversial. There are some who say it existed; however, there really is no proof."

Dance historian and master instructor of Oriental dance *Hadia*, also known as *Joselina* when performing Flamenco, confirmed this to me in a phone conversation one evening. She explained that through research, she had arrived at the same conclusion. In any case, its tempo is somewhat difficult to dance as it has a slightly monotonous and slow rhythm. There is little if any similarity between Belly or Oriental Dance and Flamenco. However, the two combined do make for an exciting fusion piece. Flamenco travel steps and distinctive turns are incorporated with such Oriental moves as shimmies, undulations, and small hip circles. The dancer performs to Arabicized rumbas and Spanish-Arabic songs from the many fusion artists of today such as the former French-based group known as *Alabina* as well as *Elissa* from Lebanon and another of my personal favorites, *Hakim* from Casablanca who is based in Málaga. A popular Flamenco duo of the seventies that incorporated Arabic influences was Lole y Manuel. This came naturally to the married couple as Lole, who sang in both Spanish and Arabic, was born in Seville to a Moroccan mother, and Manuel, who played the guitar, was born in the North African Spanish enclave of Ceuta.

The author at Djinn Show 2002, photo by Lucie Vendettoli

The fusion dancer wears a combination of an Oriental and Flamenco costume such as a full skirt ruffled at the edges, embellished with a hip belt or scarf. The skirt is used as a prop by manipulating it into graceful forms to the rhythm of the music while accentuating moves and adorning the dance, as in Flamenco. An Oriental bra or short blouse is worn that bares the midriff, and accessories such as a red flower in the hair and large hooped Gypsy earrings complete the look.

This type of fusion performance (when done well) is very enthusiastically received by audiences. The appeal of this fusion dance is steadily rising and lies in the fact that both styles merge superbly, in music, dance, and in costume. Think of the strong fire and earth masculine elements of Flamenco complimented by the soft air and water of feminine Oriental dance.

Oriental dancer and instructor Maria Amaya of New Mexico demonstrates and teaches Spanish/Arabic fusion steps that she identifies as "Zambra" in her award-winning documentary on Granada titled *Gypsy Fire*. Another one of my favorite instructors is Spanish-born Pilar Sanchez, known professionally as *Puella Lunaris*. Through her instructional video *Zambra Flamenca*, she explains its history as well as teaching and demonstrating a full Zambra choreography to the music of Quintero, León, and Quiroga. By popularizing the art from through her videos, her goal is to save the tradition of the Zambra from the danger of extinction.

Flamenco-Arabe dance also allows belly dancers to perform a barefoot version of Flamenco without having to undergo years of training in complex footwork and heelwork. On the other hand, I have seen little if any interest at all in Flamenco dancers performing such fusion pieces. This likely also has to do with the fact that, as it is performed barefoot, Flamenco dancers would have to forsake the intricate heelwork they spent years mastering — it is fundamental to their art.

La Chunga

One barefoot Flamenco dancer was *La Chunga*, born Micaela Flores Amaya in 1938 to Gypsy parents in Marseilles. Her longtime friend and art representative Britt Jeppsson informed me that the sister of "Chunga's" mother was none other than Carmen Amaya. Born into a gifted family, La Chunga was raised in Barcelona and danced barefoot since she was a child of six years old, true to Flamenco's roots. Her specialty was the lively Rumba Flamenca and she often wore modest Gypsy blouses, sometimes baring her midriff with skirts that came to be her trademark. La Chunga was and still is a beautiful Spanish woman with an artistic personality that was characterized by her unconventional originality. My parents remember seeing a young La Chunga dancing barefoot for money on the streets of Madrid during the 1950s, in her simple everyday house dress.

In 1970, she starred in the Spanish film *Ley De Raza* (The Law of the Race). The movie opens with La Chunga dancing in the countryside as she marks the rhythm with her mouth, lip-synching to lyrics that only she can hear. Her facial expression is intense showing extreme confidence, attitude, defiance, and concentration as she dances barefoot in a proud and confident style with hip sways, small hip circles, and figures 8s while stomping and stepping back and forth. She turns and jumps with jazz hands and then proceeds to trace firm and invisible circles in the air with her wrists and fingers.

As she gained in popularity, La Chunga eventually adjusted her style and appearance to a more marketable Flamenco look in order to increase her appeal to a wider audience. She eventually took up painting and became a respected artist of this genre as well. La Chunga approached this art just as she did dancing, impulsively and without any formal training. She has been exhibiting her work since the early sixties in France and Spain and at the time of this writing, her works are currently being displayed at Galería de Arte Eboli in Madrid. Pablo Ruiz Picasso once said about her: "How can it be possible that a Gypsy girl without studies expresses such sensibility and color in her paintings...?"

THE MUSIC

Zambra Mora is considered a rare form of Flamenco; however, it is more influenced by Arabic melodies than any other form of Spanish music. Zambra Mora rhythm is often described as a form of tango with Arabic flavor, most likely derived from Muslim and Mozárabic chants. The guitar's sixth string is detuned down to D and the tempo can be somewhat repetitive due to its continuous binary rhythm. It has a 4/4 rhythm; *1 2 3 4 - 1 2 3 4 - 1 2 3 4* or *tum ta-ta-ta* with emphasis on the first beat. It is played in mid range with one note in the upper register and another in the lower. The result is a haunting Arabic melody over an underlying repetitive bass-like guitar structure. Renowned Flamenco dancer, choreographer and guitarist Simón el Rubio also explains it as a 2/4 rhythm with accent on the first beat; *1 2 - 1 2 - 1 2*. He added that "it is not frequently played within today's Flamenco circles."

This style of Flamenco was popularized by grand master Sabicas (1912-1990), who composed such music under the titles "Danza Mora" and "Danza

Arabe." Sabicas, known as the "King of Flamenco," was not the first to play this style, but he did develop and popularize it while incorporating a more Arabic feel as it became one his great signature solo pieces. However, Carmen Amaya's father *El Chino* is believed to be the first guitarist to perform Zambra Mora on guitar — about 15 years prior to Sabicas. Other talented guitarists have also performed Zambra Mora, to include Esteban de Sanlúcar (1910-1989), who also composed Danza Mora. Carlos Montoya (1903-1993), nephew of Ramón Montoya, who performs an evocative "Zambra," Juan Serrano (1934) and Paco Peña (1942), both from Córdoba, also recorded brilliant and moving compositions of Danza Mora and Zambra Mora respectively. Liona Boyd (1949), known as the "First Lady of the Guitar," studied under Andrés Segovia (1893-1987) and captures the rhythm of Zambra Mora in her "Moorish Dance" piece. Francisco Tárrega (1852-1909) also wrote a very moving, medieval flavored *Danza Mora* while *Ojos de Brujo*, a popular band from Barcelona who call their music "hip hop flamenco," recorded a song titled "*Zambra*" in 2002 that begins with the pulsating Zambra Mora rhythm.

Master Egyptian percussionist Hossam Ramzy collaborated with Flamenco guitarist Rafa el Tachuela to produce an album titled "Flamenco Arabe" in 2003. This work celebrates and combines the three musical cultures of India, the Middle East, and Andalusia. The piece called "Silk Route" begins with a Kathak number, followed by an Egyptian and a Flamenco track, revealing the Hindu influence of the latter two styles while telling the story of their migration from their home in India as they traveled to Egypt and Spain. The trilogy culminates with a Spanish Rumba incorporating Indian and Arabic musical styles.

"Zambra" is now used to refer the Zambra Mora rhythm in Flamenco guitar. At an outdoor Flamenco show in the perfumed gardens of the Alcázar de los Réyes Cristianos in Córdoba's old quarter, a talented local guitarist ended his set with what he introduced as a Zambra solo. He began to detune the 6th string and performed a brilliant, rarely heard Zambra Mora piece, to my delight and that of the entire audience.

Zambra Mora has an earthy, dramatic, and hypnotic rhythm with a slow, steady beat that often speeds up in tempo as the song ends. Sometimes the rhythm was kept by striking two pieces of bronze together, as in one of Carmen Amaya's versions of "La Tana." Although not much recognized as a singer, she was an electrifying dancer, and Carmen Amaya captured the raw energy and emotion of the Gypsies through her voice. She recorded few songs and my favorite in particular is "La Tana" (like *Tani*, it is short for "Gitana.")

The song begins with the rhythmic strumming of the Zambra Mora guitar as Carmen begins accompanying with pitos. As the rhythm slowly builds momentum, she begins her tacóneo. A cantaór shouts in the background: "Viva el Moro, el Moro!!!" As she and the guitarist reach a peak, the music then slows down and she solemnly begins to sing:

Mi madre se llamo Tana desde la pila de su bautismo,
Y yo por nacer gitana, el padre cura me puso lo mismo.
Al compás de palillos y guitarra a este mundo vine yo
Y me truje toda la gracia de la tribu Faraón.
Nací donde quiso Dio, mi cuna una canasta
Porque dicen que soy una gitana sincera.

My mother was called Tana ever since the basin of her baptism,
And since I was born a Gypsy, the father-priest named me the same
To the rhythm of castanets and guitars, into this world I came
And I brought with me all the charm of the Pharaon tribe.
I was born where God wished, my crib was a basket.
For they say that I am a true Gypsy.

Although the Zambra Mora rhythm is seldom performed or heard today in music circles, the traditional Zambra Gitana remains strong and persists as an integral part of the tourism industry that remains exclusive to Granada and to none of the other seven provinces of Andalusia.

8. ANDALUSIA

The former Kingdoms of Castile and Aragón were united as one country by the year 1516, and 45 years later Madrid was selected as the capital of Spain due to its almost exact central location. In 1833, Andalusia was divided into its current eight provinces out of a total of fifty that formed the country.

It is the largest of the seventeen independent regions that were formed after the drafting of the Spanish Constitution of 1978; it became an autonomous region in 1982. Partly due to its geographical location, the southern region of Spain has always preserved its unique character and heritage.

Here the Mediterranean and the Atlantic unite at the Straits of Gibraltar, where Spain and Morocco are separated by just about ten miles. As a gateway linking Europe to Africa, Gibraltar has always attracted diverse people and cultures throughout the centuries. The region has been shaped by Iberians, Phoenicians, Celts, Greeks, Carthaginians, Romans, Vandals, Visigoths, Jews, Syrians, Arabs, and Berbers.

Andalusia contains 105 municipalities with a population of 7.4 million in 2006. Spanning nearly a quarter of the country, it covers an area of 87,000 kilometers. Each of the eight provinces has its capital named after it. The overall capital of Andalusia is Seville, with the highest population at nearly 2 million inhabitants. The province with the smallest population is Huelva, with approximately 142,000 residents.

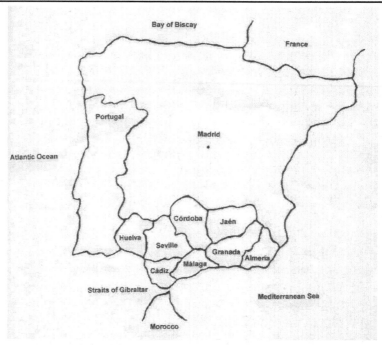

Map of Spain, Showing the Provinces of Andalusia

According to the Spanish National Institute of Statistics, the population of Spain in 2005 was 43.1 million. The Muslim population has been estimated between 500,000 to 1,000,000, thus constituting 2.3% of the country's population at most. The Federation of Spanish Islamic Entities agrees to a figure close to one million legal and illegal Muslim immigrants living in Spain today that are predominantly Moroccan. Granada is home to one of the largest Islamic communities in the country with over 15, 000 Muslims.

I wonder what Charles Martel would say about the estimated nearly 10% Muslim population in France today, the largest in Western Europe.

In the Latin Quarter of Paris on the banks of the Seine River, at Place Muhammad V, stands the *Institut du Monde Arabe* (Institute of the Arab World). The cultural center pays homage to the Muslim civilization from its beginnings to the present throughout its 22 Arab countries. Past and present are also reflected in its outer construction as the latest technology and traditional Arabic architecture are combined. The southern façade facing the courtyard displays modern steel elements and ornamental Islamic latticework known as *musharabiya*. These geometric designs control the amount of sunlight that enters the building through thousands of small light sensitive shutters that open and close according to the amount of sunlight sensed.

Built in 1987 from glass, cement, and aluminum, the impressive structure houses a library, cinema, language school, 300-seat hall, gift shop, temporary exhibitions, restaurants, an audio visual center and a fascinating museum located on the 4th, 6th, and 7th floors. It is on the 4th floor that Andalusí treasures are exhibited. Tapestries, parchments, sculptures, artwork, ceramics, Koranic calligraphy, astrolabes, ancient costumes, jewelry, and bas-reliefs can all be admired at Arab World Institute tracing the history of the Islamic and Pre-Islamic world.

Institut du Monde Arabe, Paris, France

In June 2006, French President Jacques Chirac inaugurated a memorial to the estimated 50,000 Muslim soldiers who fought for France and gave their lives at Verdun and other battle grounds during World War I. The elegant and traditional white Moorish-style monument came at a cost of 500,000 euros. The unveiling of the monument was the high point of the commemorations marking the 90th anniversary of the bloody Battle of Verdun in France.

Andalusia is the largest region of Spain in terms of population and of the estimated 50 million people who visit Spain each year, roughly half chose Andalusia for their vacation destination. The Costa del Sol (the Sunshine Coast or Coast of the Sun) area of Andalusia is favored by German and British residents, who have second homes throughout the region, selected for its sunny climate, extensive Mediterranean beaches, and laid back, relaxed atmosphere.

Southern Spain has much to offer to its visitors: a unique ambiance, contrasting landscapes, enchanting medieval villages, palatial architecture, and magnificent historical sites. There is something for everybody: snow-capped mountain ranges, a myriad of cultural activities, miles of sun-drenched golden beaches, and sunny skies with an extraordinary climate. Its essence is captured in the region's slogan: *"Andalucía — sólo hay una"* ("Andalusia, there is only one").

Traces of Arab cultures have survived throughout Andalusia, be it in architecture, art, landscape, language, music, song, dance, or cuisine — all serving as wonderful reminders of the greatness the Moors once achieved in the land of Spain.

Almería

There is a saying about this province that captures its history: *Cuando Almería era Almería, Granada era su alquería*, translated as "When Almería was Almería, Granada was its farmhouse."

Alcazába in Almería

Almería was already established as a significant Mediterranean port during Roman times, when it was known as *Urci*. Founded in 955 by Abd al-Rahman III, it is considered to be one of the best preserved Andalusian cities in terms of Moorish heritage. During the 10th century, Almería was the most important seaport of the Iberian Peninsula. Merchants from all over

Europe and the Middle East came to do business at the markets here, once considered to be the best in Moorish Spain. Almería fell to the Christians in December of 1489; Granada itself, the last remaining Moorish kingdom, was to be conquered but two years later.

Overlooking the city stands the alcazába, a magnificent 10th century fortress built high upon a hill over the ruins of an earlier fort by Abderahman III.

Construction was commissioned in 955 by Abd al-Rahman III and the complex was expanded by his successors. The alcazába contained houses, baths, a mosque, an artillery store, and water storage units known as *aljíbes*. There is a reconstructed Moorish house or apartment where one can really experience what home life must have been like over ten centuries ago. This alcazába is regarded as the largest Muslim fortification in Spain, where fantastic views of the city and port can be taken in.

Legend has it that during the 11th century, the favorite Moorish slave girl of the poet king *al-Mu'tasim* (1052-1091), named *Galiana*, died by a particular window of the alcazába. One day, the young Galiana heard a handsome Christian prisoner sing and she became totally captivated by his melodic voice and charmed by his looks. Wanting nothing more than to liberate him, she tried to help the prisoner escape by climbing out from her window. Startled, and spotted by the guards, he chose to plunge to his death rather than be re-captured. Another version has it that he accidentally fell to his death. A few days later, Galiana died of sadness, leaning upon the very sill of this window that is known as *La Ventana de la Odalisca* (The Concubine's Window).

Ventana de la Odalisca, Almería

Los Aljíbes de Jayrán or the Wells of Jayrán are another impressive site to behold. These underground chambers for collecting, storing, and distributing water were built under the order of King Jayrán during the early 11th century to supply water to the city. The king commissioned a channel for this purpose of about four miles in length that passed underneath the town. Due to its excellent acoustics, private Flamenco shows are held here under the name of *Peña El Taranto*, a society for members and aficionados. The impressive *Muralla de Jayrán* or Wall of Jayrán connects the alcazába to the *Cerro de San Cristobal* or Hill of San Cristobal.

The *Plaza Vieja* in the center of the town is where the old Arab market was situated long ago. Nearby is the famous *Barrio de La Chanca*, the Gypsy quarter known for its cave dwellings with brightly painted façades. This residential area situated below the alcazába has been home to the Gypsies and fishermen of Almería for centuries.

Almería has the hottest temperatures in Andalusia with over 300 days of sunshine a year. About 25 miles north of the city you will encounter rocky scenery and a barren landscape in the village of *Tabernas*, Europe's only true desert region or sub-desert land. Here lies the location shoot of many "spaghetti western" films such as "A Fistful of Dollars" and "The Good, the Bad and the Ugly," as well as other classics like "Lawrence of Arabia" and "Cleopatra." Many of the film sets have remained on location and can now be visited as tourist attractions at three separate theme parks.

CÁDIZ

Cádiz may be the oldest city in Western Europe. Founded by the Phoenicians around 1100 BCE, its antiquity is proudly reflected in the city's slogan, *"La Ciudad Trimilenia* (The Tri-millennium City).

Cádiz, located on the Atlantic side of the peninsula, was conquered by the Christians in 1262. Considered a major port city in southern Spain, it was also the departure point of the second and fourth voyage of Christopher Columbus (or Cristóbal Colón as he is known to Spaniards), as he headed west and "discovered the New World," America, a land that had already been discovered by Basque fishermen and others decades and possibly centuries before, but which was kept a tight secret for the abundance of superior fishing that the region yielded.

Cathedral in Cádiz

The cathedral is the most impressive landmark in Cádiz and stands as one of the largest and oldest in Spain. When approached from a distance on the Paseo Marítimo, it looks somewhat Arabian in style with its golden, tiled dome and huge towers.

1st Century BCE Roman Ruins in Cádiz

The Baroque and Neo-Classical cathedral was built upon the original 13th century structure that was destroyed late in the 16th century; this re-construction did not begin until the late 18th century and was not completed until the mid 19th century. The equally magnificent interior houses the tomb of Manuel de Falla, a native composer of Cádiz.

Nearby lie the ruins of the oldest and best preserved Roman theater in the country; it was discovered in 1980. Judging by its dimensions it may have been the second largest of its kind, possibly holding an audience of up to 25,000 spectators. The theater was built during the 1st century BCE in honor of Julius Caesar who visited Cádiz around 45 BCE.

Next to the cathedral you will find a 13th century gate known as *Arcos de la Rosa*, constructed by Alfonso X. This was the second gate to the city that was once encircled by a protective wall.

13th Century Arco de la Rosa in Cádiz

The palatial *al-cázar* in the town of Jeréz de la Frontera north east from the city of Cádiz is one of the few and finest examples of 12th century Almohad architecture that remain, although major additions were incorporated during the 18th century.

Alcázar Gate at Jeréz de la Frontera

Jeréz de la Frontera is known worldwide for its delicious sherry. This type of sweet wine has been produced here since the Phoenicians first introduced the Palomino grape over 3000 years ago and it continues to be a strong export to this day. Jeréz is not only where sherry was first cultivated, but is also well known for its wonderful Andalusian dancing horse exhibitions and is recognized as one of the original centers where Flamenco was cultivated.

In the heart of Cádiz between the sea and mountains lies the historic and artistic town of Medina Sidonia. This town was once a Roman colony known as *Asido Caesarina*, mentioned by Pliny. The colony was built over a Phoenician settlement known *Bulla Assido*, situated 300 meters above sea level. Under Visigoth rule it was the capital of the province and when the Moors arrived in 712, it became the capital of the *Sidonia Cora*, or *Sadunia*, until it was conquered by the Catholic Kings in 1264.

CÓRDOBA

This town was founded by the Romans during the 2nd century BCE and became the first Roman colony in the Iberian Peninsula. Its strategic location by the Guadalquivir River made it a most significant city. Such commodities as wheat, olive oil, and wine were frequently imported to Rome from Córdoba.

El Puente Romano (The Roman Bridge) that stretches over the Guadalquivir was built by Emperor Augustus during the first century BCE. This impressive bridge consisting of 16 arches once formed a part of the *Via Augusta*, the largest roadway that the Romans built in the Iberian Peninsula. According to ancient chronicles, when the Moors arrived they found the bridge in complete ruins and in 719, the Caliphate of Damascus ordered its reconstruction.

1ˢᵗ Century BCE Roman Bridge in Córdoba

At the southern end of the Roman Bridge stands the *Torre de la Calahorra*, or *Calahorra Tower*. This monument that originally consisted of two towers linked by a gated arch was built by the Moors during the 10ᵗʰ century. The purpose of the tower was to protect against invasions arriving from the Roman Bridge over the Guadalquivir. It was completely rebuilt by the Christians during the 14ᵗʰ century and it stands today as the oldest defense building in Córdoba.

The old Jewish quarter, typically known as the *Barrio de la Judería*, with its maze of narrow streets, colorful patios, floral balconies, charming shops and cafés, has been recently restored. As far back as the Roman era, the Judería has been a significant quarter. The most impressive historic monument in the Judería, in fact in Córdoba, is the Great Mosque, formerly known as *La Mezquita* or *Great Mosque of Aljama* that was converted into a cathedral in 1236 and recently — questionably — renamed *La Santa Iglesia Catedral* (The Holy Cathedral Church). This masterpiece is the only one of its kind in Europe.

Lateral Door of the Mosque in Córdoba

Torre de la Calahorra in Córdoba

Construction began by Abd al-Rahman I in 785 and true to tradition it was greatly expanded for over two centuries by his successors, Abd al-Rahman II in 833, al Hakam II in 961 and al-Mansur in 987. The 850-columned mosque was inspired by another in Damascus and like many other great buildings, was originally built on the site of a former Roman temple and Visigoth basilica. The interior pillars were constructed from columns used in Roman and Visigoth buildings in Spain, France, Constantinople, and Carthage. This stunning work of Arab architecture is considered one of the most magnificent Islamic buildings in the world; it was once second in size to the mosque at Mecca (this honor now goes to the recently built Hassan II Mosque in Casablanca).

Interior of La Mezquita in Córdoba

When Córdoba was conquered by the Christians in 1236, the mosque was converted into a cathedral and its first Catholic mass was held that year on June 29. Modification and additions continued for nearly three centuries. In 1523, extensive remodeling was entrusted to local architect Hernán Ruiz, who was charged with modifying the original works of Abd al-Rahman III and al-Mansur by transforming the cathedral into Gothic style. The project continued until the beginning of the 17th century under his son and grandson, Hernán Ruiz II and Hernán Ruiz III. The result was an architectural masterpiece combining Muslim, Gothic, Byzantine, Baroque, and Renaissance elements that earned its title of World Heritage Site by UNESCO.

Another declared World Heritage Site is the *Alcázar de los Reyes Cristianos.* The royal palace or alcázar existed as a fortress during Roman times and is now a palace with magnificent gardens dotted with ponds, cypresses, orange and lemon trees as well as trickling fountains carved of stone, and towering palm trees.

Gardens of the Alcázar de los Reyes in Córdoba

The alcázar was greatly reconstructed in 1328 by King Alfonso XI (also known as "The Vengeful") and was rebuilt in a European Gothic style in order to introduce the city to a new form that contrasted with the Muslim architecture that had dominated for centuries. The Royal Baths, situated on the lower level, were constructed in classic Arabian style. There is now an entrance fee into the alcázar that includes admission to the 10th century Caliphal Baths nearby, which the evidence indicates were in use well into the 13th century by Almohad rulers.

At a smaller tower of the alcázar, victims of the Spanish Inquisition were publicly hanged. The fortress became a civil, then later a military, prison during the 19th to mid 20th century. Now during the summer Flamenco performances by talented local artists are given during the evenings at the Royal Gardens, with the Christian Alcázar serving as the most perfect backdrop. Córdoba is a strong candidate for becoming the Ciudad Europea de la Cultura 2016 (European Cultural City of 2016) — as it was over a thousand years ago.

During the 10th century, Abd al-Rahman III is reported to have had over 3500 women in his royal harem. His favorite was named *Zahra* and legend has it that he was so enamored of her that in the year 936 he began construction of a Caliphal residence and city as a tribute to her, with the wealth she left him when she died; it was truly fit for a queen. The urban center and largest city in the entire region, was founded in 940 about five miles west of the city of Córdoba. Abd al-Rahman III named it *Madinat az-Zahra*, meaning "City of Zahra" or "City of the Orange Blossom," in her honor and it is known in Spanish as *Medina Azahara*.

Ruins of Medina Azahara in Córdoba

Medina Azahara or *Ciudad Vieja* (Old City), as it was also known, was constructed with such costly materials as gold, ebony, ivory, marble, stucco, onyx, and jasper. Over 4,300 imported marble and jasper columns were used in its construction. The complex was comprised of three terraces; the top terrace overlooked the city that was reserved as the Caliphal residence, the middle floor held the government and administrative offices as well as apartments for the senior court officials, and the lower level was where the common folk lived and congregated.

One particularly luxurious room was known as the *Salón Rico* or "rich room." It is said to have been decorated with an abundance of jewels set within the floral wall decorations. In the middle of this room stood a big fountain filled with mercury that reflected the rays of sunlight. Legend has it that when Abd al-Rahman III wanted to impress his guests, his servants would shake the surface of the inside the fountain and the entire room became illuminated by the glittering sparkles of mercury.

Medina Azahara came to symbolize the new political power and ideological order. Thousands of people were employed within this spectacular community, as eunuchs, musicians, and male and female servants. The stables were big enough to accommodate 2000 horses, and over 4000 servants waited in the palace. It contained 300 baths, a zoo, an aviary, several large fish ponds, bath houses, perfumed gardens, bejeweled fountains, pools, patios, and 400 houses. There were also mosques, schools, pavilions, barracks, and even weapon factories. An aqueduct was built to carry water from the Sierra Morena Mountains to the city. It is believed to have taken over 10,000 men, 2,600 mules, 400 camels, and 25 years to build this once magnificent city that was only comparable to the royal residence of Baghdad and Damascus.

However, the fate of this Muslim residence was to become a prison for Abd al-Rahman III as his power began to wane and in 1010, his beloved city was destroyed and burned to the ground by rampaging Berbers. Documented descriptions and excavations conducted during the last century have provided a good idea of its original structure and appearance since its discovery in 1911. Presently, it is still being restored due to years of abandonment, destruction, ransacking and the removal of its parts for use in the construction of other buildings. The archeological remains that are seen today are only about a tenth of what once existed within Medina Azahara.

Ruins of Medina Azahara

Another Caliphal city was built by al-Mansur and named *Madinat al-Zahi-ra*, meaning "City of Brilliance." Construction of this rivaling palace, situated by the river about a mile east of the capital, took place between 979 and 981. Like Medina Azahara, it was surrounded by walls and contained a mosque, government office, and public facilities. However, it stood for only three decades until it too was destroyed by Berbers in 1009.

GRANADA

There is an oft-quoted saying written by Spanish poet *Francisco de Icaza* that captures the essence and beauty of this town: "Give him alms, woman, for there is nothing more tragic in life than to be a blind man in Granada." An Arab proverb says, "God gives to those he loves a means of living in Granada." It is without a doubt the most Arabian-influenced town in Spain, where traces of Moorish history remains vibrantly abundant. During the Nasrid Dynasty, Granada was one of the largest and affluent cities in medieval Europe and was the last capital of al-Andalus from 1248 to 1492. The Moors were most fond of Granada and to this day, their loss continues to be mourned.

Possibly the oldest surviving Moorish building in Granada is the *Corral de Carbón* (Coal Yard), built in 1336 as an alhóndiga or guesthouse, that was also used as a merchant shop where goods were deposited, bought, and sold.

Originally known as *Alhóndiga Yidida*, it was built under the command of the Nasrid ruler Yusuf I, who ruled Granada from 1333 to 1354, as a hostel and warehouse for Arab merchants situated in front of the Alcaizería crossing Zacatín Street.

Entrance to the Corral de Carbón in Granada

A horseshoe arch adorns the entrance leading out to a central patio that opens into several rooms. It stands as the only fully conserved Arab structure of its kind in the country. The building received its present name from the Christians during the 16th century when coal traders lodged here and it was also used as a coal yard where coal was weighed. During the same century, theater plays were performed for the public and it was known as *Corral de Comedias;* and during the 17ᵗʰ century it functioned as a tenement house. Until 2004 it served as a tourism office and it currently houses a craft and souvenir shop while the tourist center has been moved to nearby Plaza Santa Ana.

Possibly the last construction of Arabian architecture is the mid 15ᵗʰ century Nasrid *Palacio de Dalahorra*. Located in the Albayzín, with spectacular views of the Alhambra, it is here where Sultana *Aixa*, Boabdil's demanding mother, resided. The palace is open to the public and well worth seeing with its fine Mudéjar ceiling.

Patio of Palacio de Dalahorra in Granada

While the Gypsies settled in the Sacromonte area, the Moors made their homes in the Albayzín or Arab quarter of Granada. This residential area, declared a World Heritage Site by UNESCO, is linked through a labyrinth of narrow alleyways and cobbled streets dotted with charming whitewashed houses. These small private villas enclosed in secluded gardens and orchards are known as *Cármenes*. The Albayzín was the private residence of the wealthy Moors between the 12ᵗʰ and 15ᵗʰ centuries.

Shopping in the Alcaicería, Zacatín, and Calderería streets is a unique cultural experience while the Plaza Santa Ana is a delightful area to spend an afternoon. However, by far the most important Arabian landmark in Spain and best preserved example of medieval Moorish architecture in Europe is the magnificent Arabian palace-fortress known as the *Alhambra*.

The Alhambra

This architectural masterpiece originally stood as a Muslim fortress during the 9th century and was greatly expanded and completed during 13th century. The Alhambra was the residence of the Nasrid Dynasty who ruled Granada for nearly two and a half centuries.

The Alhambra complex is comprised of the *Palacios Nazaries* (Nasrid Royal Palace), the *alcazába* (fortress or military zone) and the royal gardens and summer retreat known as *Generalife*. The foundation of the alcazába goes as far back as the Visigoths who built the city walls which, therefore, are the Alhambra's oldest remaining section.

This royal palace and fortress of a reddish hue, set against a backdrop of snowcapped peaks of the Sierra Nevada Mountain range that overlooks the city, was once home to the sultans and harems of Granada long ago. This magical place features bubbling fountains, trickling streams, slender columns, myrtle hedges, elaborate patios, fresh plants, and floral gardens that are symmetrically designed. Exquisite glazed tiles adorn the walls and meticulously clipped trees decorate the grounds. Strategic lookout points to the city were carefully constructed within the walls where impressive views can be enjoyed. A full day is needed to absorb its magical ambience. Breathtaking views of the city and Alhambra from the lookout point at Albayzín's highest point of *Plaza de San Nicholás* can best be appreciated during sunset.

The Alhambra is decorated with poetic verses written by *Ibn Zamrak* of the 14th century, the last of the great Hispanic-Muslim poets of al-Andalus. Although he was not the only poet to contribute to the Alhambra, he was considered the most brilliant of all. This poem appears in *La Sala de Dos Hermanas* (The Hall of the Two Sisters) that has been translated into Castilian by Emilio García Gómez.

> Las columnas en todo son tan bellas,
> Que en lenguas corredoras anda su fama:
> Lanza el mármol su clara luz, que invade
> La negra esquina que tizno la sombra;
> Irisan sus reflejos, y dirías
> Son, a pesar de su tamaño, perlas.
> Jamás vimos alcázar más excelso,
> De contornos más claros y espaciosos.
> Jamás vimos jardín más floreciente,
> De cosecha más dulce y más aroma.

> The columns in all are so lovely,
> That its fame is spread abroad in many languages:
> Casting in marble its clear light that invades
> The black corners tarnished by shade;
> Iridescent are its reflections and one would say
> They are, despite their size, pearls.
> Never have we seen an Alcázar more sublime,
> Or contours more clear and spacious.
> Never have we seen a garden more flourishing,
> Or a sweeter, more aromatic harvest.

Many wonderful sites surround the complex including the open-air courts of the *Patio de Los Arrayanes* (Courtyard of Myrtle) and the *Patio de Los Leones* (Courtyard of the Lions) that was once the royal harem. The frequently photographed *Fountain of the Lions* is made of white marble and is considered one the highlights of Muslim sculpture. Its twelve meticulously sculpted lions with spouts pouring water from their mouths date back to the 14th century, however some parts are as old as the 11th century.

Engraved upon the rim of the fountain is an inscription also written by *Ibn Zamrak*; it reads,

> En apariencia, agua y mármol parecen confundirse,
> sin que sepamos cuál de ambos se desliza.
> ¿No ves cómo el agua se derrama en la taza
> pero sus caños la esconden enseguida?

In its appearance, water and marble seem to mingle,
Without knowing which of the two flows through
Do you not see how the water pours from the basin?
But is immediately hidden by its spouts?

Fountain of the Patio de Los Leones at the Alhambra

Streams and fountains of soothing water can be seen and heard in abundance within the Alhambra, as the Moors held the sound of bubbling or trickling water in the highest regard due to their homeland being dry and waterless. Washington Irving wrote on this subject in his *Tales of the Alhambra*: "An abundant supply of water, brought from the mountains by old Moorish aqueducts, circulates throughout the palace, supplying its baths and fish-pools, sparkling in jets within its halls or murmuring in the channels along the marble pavements. When it has paid its tribute to the royal pile and visited its gardens and pastures, it flows down the long avenue leading to the city, tinkling in rills, gushing in fountains and maintaining a perpetual verdure in those groves that embower and beautify the whole hill of the Alhambra."

Irving occupied several rooms in the Alhambra for three months while writing his romantic novel in 1829. At this time the Alhambra had been in an abandoned state, home to Gypsies, beggars, stray dogs, and cats. Inspired by the ghosts and spirits of sultans and oriental dancing girls of long ago, Irving's book opened the eyes of the world to the Alhambra and as a result, over two million visitors each year marvel at its wonder. Naturally, this palace has also inspired many love songs.

The Alhambra

"Vivir in Cuento de Hada"

Habibi ya ghaali
M' saharni layali...
Vivir un cuento de hadas danos la mano
Tu me llevaste a L'Alambra hace mil años
Lo fuimos por un sueño, sueño encantado
Tu eras la princesa en L'Alambra; yo, tu fiel enamorado
Tú paseabas, tú paseabas y yo con mi silencio te enamoraba
Y era tu dueño, y era tu dueño y tu paloma mía, volaba el sueño
No te vayas del sueño jamás despierte
Siéntate aquí con migo junto a una fuente, junto a una fuente...

My love, my dear precious love
You who leave me sleepless every night
To live within a fairy tale, let us hold hands
You took me to the Alhambra one thousand years ago
We traveled in a dream, an enchanted dream
You were the princess of the Alhambra, I was truly in love with
   you

You strolled by and I with my silence made you fall in love with me
And I was your master, and you my white dove, flew within the
dream
Do not leave the dream, never awaken
Sit here with me by the fountain, by the fountain...

Overlooking the grounds of the Alhambra is the early 14ᵗʰ-century *Generalife*, a stunning complex adorned with fountains, elaborate pools, intricate
fountains, small ponds, aromatic flowers, and plush gardens. Serving as the
summer residence of the Nasrid Dynasty, the inspiration behind its design
and construction was the Koranic version of Paradise.

Among the many highlights within the Generalife grounds is the stunning
patios or courtyards such as the *Patio de la Acequia* (Courtyard of the Stream)
and *Patio del Ciprés de la Sultana* (Courtyard of the Cypress of the Sultana).

Patio de La Sultana at Generalife

Legend has it that it was under a special tree within this courtyard that
Zoraya, the favorite wife within Boabdil's harem, secretly met her lover, who
happened to be a knight of the rivaling *Abencerraje* family or *Banu Sarraj*. According to legend, all the male Abencerrajes of the family were executed under Boabdil's orders when he discovered the couple together. The massacre
is said to have taken place at a banquet held in the magnificent *Salon de los*

Abencerrajes (Hall of the Abencerrajes), where the throats of 36 men of this noble Arab family were slit while Boabdil watched their blood flow into the Fountain of Lions. Many believe that there was no secret romance and that the slaughter was a conspiracy plotted by a rival family known as *Los Zenetes,* who concocted the story of the relationship between Zoraya and a member of the Abencerrajes in order to provoke Boabdil's reaction.

Once Granada was taken by the Catholic Kings, Boabdil, the last Muslim ruler, is believed to have left the Alhambra complex through the *Torre de los Siete Suelos* (Tower of the Seven Floors). His wishes were duly respected when he ordered it to be blocked off and never to be used again.

View of the Alhambra from the Patio of the New Mosque in Granada

Not surprisingly, the Alhambra and the Generalife are also declared Word Heritage Sites by UNESCO. The Alhambra is also one of the 21 final candidates selected to be named one of the New Seven Wonders of the World in 2007 under a program organized by a Swiss-based corporation. Other spectacular man-made structures that are hopeful contenders include the Acropolis in Athens, the Great Wall in China, the Coliseum in Rome, the Eiffel Tower in Paris, the Kremlin in Moscow, the Taj Mahal in India, Stonehenge in the UK, and the Statue of Liberty in New York.

In the summer of 2003, the first mosque in Granada was inaugurated since the days of the Reconquest over 500 years ago. The white brick building and red-tiled roof with its public extensive gardens is found in the old

Moorish quarter of Albayzín upon the hill directly facing the Alhambra at Plaza San Nicolás.

The friendly caretaker informed me that it was the culmination of a long and expensive process that lasted 22 years, mainly financed by the United Arab Emirates, Libya, Morocco, and Spain. The purpose of the mosque is to provide a place of research and learning of Islamic studies and Arabic language as well as a place for worship and spiritual home to the many Muslims that live in Granada. Exhibitions and conferences are also offered at the mosque. The Spanish Islamic community hopes that it will be a step towards improving the current European perception of the Islamic faith.

One final comment on Graná (as it is often affectionately called) for visitors; beware of the famed *Tortilla de Sacromonte* (Sacromonte Omelet). Although the recipe is ancient and the flavor is supposedly exquisite, keep in mind that its major ingredient is pork, lamb or calf brain.

HUELVA

Huelva was also founded over 3000 years ago by Phoenician traders; however, few hints of its antiquity remain. Huelva became part of Córdoba's Emirate in 756 when Abd al-Rahman I came into power. It stood as an important port city for trading with northern Africa. Huelva lies on the western part of Andalusia bordering with Portugal situated on the Atlantic coastline known as the Costa de la Luz (Coast of the Light). Of all the Andalusian provinces it may be the least visited by tourists, but it does have fine Atlantic beaches with miles of unspoiled sand. This often overlooked town lacks some of the splendor of other Andalusian cities as it was badly damaged during the devastating Lisbon earthquake of 1755, which destroyed much of its architectural history.

Huelva was captured by the Christians in 1262 and is best known for being the starting point of Christopher Columbus's first travels to the New World. He sailed from the port of *Palos de la Frontera* off the coast of Huelva and across the Atlantic in 1492, the same year that the last Moorish Kingdom of Granada fell. A colossal monument dedicated to Columbus known, as the *Monumento a la Fe Descubridora* (Monument to Faith's Discovery), or *Monumento a Colón*, is the most photographed image of Huelva.

Monumento a Colón, photo by Peter van der Krogt

This town is also famous for a particular style of Andalusian dance named *Fandangos de Huelva*, a lively folk dance form for couples somewhat similar to the Sevillanas that are also performed with castanets. There are many types of Fandangos; however, those of the province of Huelva remain the most typical and popular.

About 60 miles from the seaboard of Huelva is the geological wonder of the stalactite cave with its underground lagoon known as the *Grutas de las Maravillas* (Cavern of the Wonders), in the town of Aracena situated in the Sierra Morena Mountains. It is considered one of the finest of its kind in the world.

According to local folk legend, the spirit of a beautiful yet cursed maiden lives inside this cavern. The story begins with a young woman named Julianilla who, to her mother's dismay, took a stroll each afternoon past the fountain that flowed by the foot of the hill. It was said that in just that area lived a mischievous and infamous spirit that took delight in deceiving local young women with clever words offering promises of romance and magnificent gifts.

Julianilla, being intensely curious and allured by these ruses, disregarded her mother's sound advice and one afternoon found herself in the arms of that capricious and unreliable spirit. However, once inside the cavern, her feminine charm and warm sentiments were soon met with a powerful chill as his breath blew a frozen mist of ice cold air that swept through the entire cavern, filling the confines of her palace with snow and icicles. The malicious spirit made the distressed and betrayed maiden cry so much that lakes of tears formed as a result. It was in these lakes that the scornful spirit was drowned at the hands of Julianilla's sympathetic and vengeful gnomes. And so her tears continued to form pearls and diamonds, that to this day fall rhythmically over the lakes of the cavern.

JAÉN

Settled by the Romans in 207 BCE and conquered by the Moors in 712, Jaén became an important strategic center along local caravan routes in northern al-Andalus. Jaén is also home to one of the most important and best preserved Arab baths in Spain.

Arabic Baths at Palacio Villar-dompardo in Jaén

Situated within the narrow alley-ways of the oldest part of the town, known as *La Magdalena,* these baths are the larg-est of their kind to have survived and they display some of the finest ex-amples of 11th century Moorish ar-chitecture. During the end of the 16th century, the Count of Villardompardo and Viceroy of Peru constructed his palace over the baths, which then lay hidden in the cellar until their discovery in 1913.

Upon the hilltop stands the impressive *Castle of Santa Catalina*, originally built by the 13th century Moorish king of Jaén, Al-Hamar, who created the Alhambra in Granada. Converted into a parador, magnificent views can be seen of the town from here.

Approaching Santa Catalina Castle in Jaén

This former alcazar, captured in 1246 by Fernando III on the feast day of Santa Catalina, was later reconstructed. As a result, Santa Catalina became the patron saint of Jaén and the castle bears her name. The charming old Moorish quarter of *San Juan*, along with *La Magdalena*, is well worth visiting for its charm and history.

In the village of *La Iruela* in Jaén lie the ruins of an 11th century Moorish fortress that is unusually perched on top of a vertical rock. The picturesque *Castillo La Iruela* stands as the most romantic image of Jaén.

"Castillo La Iruela" by Manuel Ruiz, 1998

Jaén is also known for one of the most important battles, which took place on July 16 in 1212. The *Battle of Las Navas de Tolosa* marked the beginning of the end of Moorish Spain as Muslim power weakened when the Almohads were defeated by Christian troops. It was in this province where the Christian forces assembled in 1492 before permanently driving the Moors out of Granada.

Jaén is surrounded by a forest of olive trees and is best known for cultivating olives and producing oil. It is now the world's leading producer of this fruit as well as its oil (or "liquid gold," as it is called). Two historical towns within this province, Úbeda and Baeza, that date back to the 9th century, have recently been declared Heritage of Humanity Sites by UNESCO.

MÁLAGA

This is one of Spain's oldest towns, already an important Phoenician, Roman, and Visigoth settlement long before it was invaded by the Moors. Phoenician traders were responsible for planting the first vineyards here and since then, Málaga has been known for its sweet wines. *Verdial* is the name of a variety of olive cultivated in Málaga that has a folkloric danced named after it. *Verdiales de Málaga* is a primitive form of the Fandango of Moorish origin.

Although Málaga played a secondary role under the Moors to cities like Córdoba, Granada, and Seville, it was a most significant port in Mediterranean trade, particularly during the Almohad era and later during the 14th century under the Nasrid rulers. In 1487 it was captured by the Christians.

Málaga is actually the smallest of the Andalusian provinces but it is the most densely settled. Málaga city is actually the capital of the Costa del Sol. Within the province of Málaga lie miles of sunny beaches on its Mediterranean coastline with such delightful tourist towns as Torremolinos, Benalmádena, Fuengirola, Marbella, and Estepona.

In the heart of the city of Málaga lies the second largest seaport in the country after Barcelona. Málaga has been a significant harbor since the times of the Phoenicians. There are many historic Moorish attractions here, including the alcazába with its wonderful gardens and the fortress known as *Castillo de Gibralfaro*.

Entrance to the Gibralfaro Castle in Málaga

The Gibralfaro Castle was built during the 14th century during the reign of Yusuf I ,over the remains of a Phoenician lighthouse and fortress later built by Abd al-Rahman III. The views from the Gibralfaro are well worth the arduous climb up.

Construction of the alcazába on the ruins of a Roman fortress originally began during the 8th century by Abd al-Rahman I. As it was mainly constructed from delicate limestone, frequent repairs have been undertaken through the years.

Alcazába in Málaga

Ruins of a 1st Century BCE Roman Theater at the foot of the Alcazába in Málaga

The most notable work was done during the Taifa period of the mid 11ᵗʰ century. In 1333, a *muralla* or walled passage was built that connected the Gibralfaro Castle to the alcazába by Yusuf I.

At the foot of the castle lie the impressive ruins of a 1ˢᵗ century BCE Roman theater that was discovered in 1951.

Evidence shows that it was last occupied during the 3rd century and may have accommodated an audience of as many 20,000 spectators. Parts of this structure were later used by the Moors in their construction of the alcazába.

Construction of a new parking lot at the Pablo Ruiz Picasso airport in Málaga has recently uncovered Roman remains of a 2nd to 4th century BCE farm as well as a necropolis dated to the 4th to 5th century AD. Málaga is also a candidate for Ciudad Europea de la Cultura 2016.

There is a white village in the mountains of Málaga that is regarded as the most picturesque town in the province. Casares is the birthplace of the Andalusian nationalist leader Blas Infante (1885-1936). Infante, known as the "father of Andalusia," wrote the lyrics to the Andalusian anthem, *La Bandera Blanca y Verde*:

> La bandera blanca y verde vuelve, tras siglos de guerra,
> A decir paz y esperanza, bajo el sol de nuestra tierra.
>
> ¡Andaluces, levantaos!
> ¡Pedid tierra y libertad!
> ¡Sea por Andalucía libre,
> España y la Humanidad!
>
> Los andaluces queremos volver a ser lo que fuimos,
> Hombres de luz, que a los hombres, alma de hombres les dimos.
>
> The white and green flag returns after centuries of war,
> Declaring peace and hope under the sun of our land.
>
> Rise Andalusians!
> Demand land and liberty!
> Be it if for Andalusia's freedom
> Spain and humanity!
>
> We Andalusians want to return to who we were,
> Enlightened men, that to them, souls of men were given.

Seville

Legend has it that Seville was founded by Hercules. It was one of the earliest Roman settlements to emerge c. 206 BCE and became the capital of the Roman province of Baética. Seville was also the first capital of al-Andalus, from 713 to 716. The town was captured by the Almoravides during the late 11th century, who made it their capital, and so it remained under the Almohads during the 12th and 13th centuries.

The present-day capital of Andalusia rose to its great heights during this period; then it was conquered by the Christians in 1248. Seville may have been the richest and most populous city in Europe during the 16th century.

Among the many picturesque splendors of Seville is the 14th century alcázar that is found where an Almohad mosque stood during the late 12th century. After the collapse of the Caliphate of Córdoba, the alcázar became the administrative center of the Almohads.

Seville is also the home of the largest Gothic cathedral in Spain and the third largest in the world. This work of art was built over the ruins of a mosque, which in turn had replaced a Visigoth church. It is considered one of the finest achievements of Gothic architecture in Europe. Inside the cathedral lies one of the several alleged tombs of Christopher Columbus. As recent as the fall of 2006, DNA research verified that at least some of his remains are authentic. The project which began in 2002 consists of using Mitochondrial DNA techniques compared to the remains analyzed of Columbus's brother, which have been matched. Spain and the Dominican Republic each claim to hold his true burial place. DNA research also needs to be done on bone fragments buried in the Dominican Republic as the body of Columbus was moved several times after his death and his remains may also lie here. However, no permission had been granted from the Dominican Republic on the grounds that they, in their Christian faith, believe that the deceased should not be disturbed.

A magnificent view of the cathedral can be seen from a courtyard of the alcázar known as the *Patio de Banderas* (Patio of Flags) in the old Jewish neighborhood of *Santa Cruz*.

Legend has it that the former Gypsy quarter of *Triana* was named after Roman emperor Trajan, who founded the city. However, others believe that it was named after Rodrigo de Triana, born in Seville in 1469. Triana was a Jewish sailor who accompanied Columbus on his ventures. It is written that he actually saw America hours before Columbus did, aboard *The Pinta*, shouting "Tierra! Tierra!" ("Land! Land!") He was never credited with the sighting and he later relocated to Africa, converting to Islam. However, if Triana was known as *Madinat al-Taryana* by the Moors, its origins clearly lie here.

This charming medieval quarter is the most picturesque section of the city with whitewashed houses and twisting narrow cobblestone streets with courtyards with cascades of flowers.

"Patio de Banderas" by Manuel Ruiz, 1951

Triana, across the Guadalquivir on its right bank, was the heart of Flamenco song and dance during the 18th century. This neighborhood was once a working class area that was home to many great Gypsy Flamenco artists. Since the Gypsies left, during the 1960s, it has been a modern city with little trace left of Flamenco and the Gypsies.

On the banks of the Guadalquivir stands the magnificent *Torre del Oro* ('Tower of the Gold') or *Burj al-Dhahab* built by the Almohads in 1220. Legend has it that gold loot and tribute was stored in the tower. Its distinctive 12-sided shape once displayed gilded tiles and it stands as one of the many military watchtowers that once formed the Almohad system of fortification.

During its day, a heavy chain ran from the this tower to another one across the river, in order to deter enemy ships from entering the harbor. Today, it stands alone and houses as a small maritime museum.

B a r r i o
Santa Cruz
in Seville

However, the most important landmark and symbol of Seville is the former Arabian minaret or *alminara*, known as *La Giralda*, "The Weathervane"
or "The Bell Tower." Standing over 300 feet high in the center of the city, La
Giralda was originally erected as a minaret in 1184 by Almohad rulers who
undertook several vast building projects in this province. The wide ramp
leading to the very top was used by these rulers, riding on horseback. The
Giralda was the first observatory to be built in Europe and is regarded as the
culmination of Almohad architecture. This structure once functioned as an

observatory for Andalusí astronomers and is believed to have been designed by *Jabir Bin Afiah*, also known as *al-Geber*, a celebrated mathematician and astronomer from Seville who lived in the 12th century.

Torre del Oro in Seville by the Guadalquivir

During the 16th century, 24 bells were installed and to the tower, *El Giraldillo*, a weathervane was added, in the form of a bronze statue representing faith, crowning the new belfry. The work was done by Hernán Ruiz II, who also worked with his father and son on the remodeling of the Mosque in Córdoba. El Giraldillo withstood the weather atop the Giralda for over 400 years; it was replaced by a copy in 1997 while the original was restored to its full glory; it now sits once again perched high upon the Giralda. Its name is derived from the Spanish term for "revolve," or *girar*, as the Giraldillo or weathervane turns with the wind.

The next chapter explores the etymology of the many Spanish words and place-names mentioned throughout the preceding chapters.

La Giralda in Seville

9. Arabisms

At one time, the spoken language of al-Andalus, for Christians and Jews alike, was Arabic — or, rather, a dialect known as Andalusí Arabic. By the 10th century, it became a distinct idiom of Arabic as many words and terms began entering the Latin-based language of Spain. Arabic was the predominant written language and by the 13th century it was the spoken language of al-Andalus. At this time, the majority of published works produced in the Mediterranean and Near Eastern world were in Arabic; it had become the international scientific language, the language of the literate population. It was largely through this medium that Arabian culture spread throughout Europe during its Dark Ages.

A vast majority of the population in southern Spain at that time was literate (fluent in Arabic), unlike the Christian-occupied areas of northern Spain, and other European countries who held on to their Latin dialects. Arabic Andalusí became an extinct language after the fall of Moorish Spain; however, it lives on in poetry and music.

Arabic struggled on in Granada as a second language for at least a century after the Reconquest. By the late 15th century, thousands of Arabic words had integrated into *Castilian (Castellano)*, the purest of Spanish languages and the official language of Spain today. Arabic is second to spoken Latin in contributing to the Spanish language. Hundreds of words that begin with *al*, the Arabic prefix equivalent to "the" or "el" and "la" in Spanish, are fine examples;

"alcalde" (mayor) from *al-qadi;* "almohada" (cushion) from *al-mikhaddah,* "algodón" (cotton) from *al-qoton,* and "azúcar" (sugar) from *as-sukkar.*

Over 1,000 names of Spanish cities and towns are of Arabic origin as well as possibly an additional 2,000 more general words. It has been estimated that about 15% of the Spanish language is derived from Arabic. These Arabisms are found in all areas of life, from architecture, literature, music, art, and cuisine to industry and commerce, mathematics, medicine, astronomy, agriculture and geography and other sciences.

Of all the world's languages (excluding those in Muslim lands), it is Spanish that contains the most Arabic word-usage. This led to the numerous Arabisms that color the Spanish language — another legacy of the Moors. As a student of Arabic with Spanish as my native language, I was naturally intrigued with this field. Determining the origins of words, or the study of etymology, has always been of particular interest; however, it can be a tricky and misleading area as wishful thinking can color conclusions — not to mention that theories or ideas in this area are difficult if not impossible to prove. There are several Spanish words whose theoretical etymology I feel it is important to mention at this point, and therefore I have devoted an entire chapter to this subject. I have only selected words and names used of Arabic origin; however, some are also derived from the Roman, Phoenician, and Greek languages.

Aceña: The name of this water-mill comes from *as-saniya;* "the lifter."

Acequia (A-theh-kya): The name of this irrigation device is derived from *as-saqiya;* "the irrigation canal" or "channel."

Ajimez (Al-hee-mez): This originates from *as-simesa;* a wooden balcony with lattice windows usually found in the harem with shutters of wood that was often arched and divided in the center by a column.

Alhambra: This is derived from *al-hamra,* meaning "the Red," as this was the color of clay extracted from the very hill it sits upon that was used to build the outer walls of the Alhambra. At the same time, its original designer Al-Hamar (The Red), founder of the Nasrid Dynasty, likely named the complex after himself.

The Alhambra

At dusk, the Alhambra seems to be bathed in a crimson-colored light as it glows under the fiery red Andalusian setting sun. Its original name is *al-Qalat al-Hamra*, "The Red Castle" or "The Red Fortress."

Albayzín (Albay-theen): This neighborhood founded by the Moors in 1228 was originally known as *Rabad al-Bayyazin*, meaning "Neighborhood of the Falconers." The town of Baeza or *al-bayyasa* in the province of Jaén was the first significant Moorish town to fall to the Christians and when its inhabitants were forced to leave, they settled in this part of Granada and named it after their hometown. After the Reconquest, many Moors made the Albayzín their home. In Spanish, the diminutive form of a name or word can be made by adding the suffix "in." Albayzín therefore can be translated as "Little Baeza."

Alcaicería (Alkay-tha-ree-a): The name of the former silk market or silk exchange is derived from *al-qaysariyya*, meaning "Place of Caesar" or "Caesar's." The Arabs named them so in order to show appreciation for being granted permission to sell silks during the reign of Byzantine Emperor Justinian of the 6th century. The only Alcaicería preserved in Spain is found by the 16th century cathedral in Granada; however it was rebuilt after a devastating fire in 1843. Walking through this labyrinth of charming streets and shops with the sweet smell of incense and exotic spices permeating the air and the sounds of rhythmic Arab drumming in the distance, one experiences the full sensory lifebeat of Granada.

Alcantarilla (Alcan-tareeya): This term for a "sewer" or "drain" is derived from *al-qantarah*, meaning "the bridge." The "illa" ending in Castilian indicates a diminutive form, therefore translating as "the little bridge." Alcantarilla is also the name of a town in the province of Murcia that still displays a huge functioning waterwheel, or *noria*, known as *La Noria de Alcantarilla*.

Alcazába (Alca-thaba): This is derived from *al-qasabah*, meaning "the fortified enclosure," and has integrated into the English language as "Casbah." For strategic purposes, these military fortress or castles were constructed upon a hill at the highest point of the city where approaching enemies could be detected from a distance, preventing surprise attacks. Alcazábas served as administrative centers and refuges for the population of al-Andalus. Many still stand today throughout Andalusia. Among the finest are those found in Almería, Granada, Jeréz de la Frontera, and Málaga.

Alcázar (Alcathar): This is derived from *al-qasar*, "the palace" or "the castle." The term actually defines a set of buildings that were surrounded by walls that stood as both a fortified palace and fortress. This building served as residence to the Emir or Caliph. There are an estimated 2,500 castles in Spain but at one time as many as 10,000 are believed to have existed. Built for control, warfare, and protection, Spain has always been the "Land of Castles" or *Castilla* (pronounced "cas-teeya"), whose natives or *Castellanos* speak the Castilian language.

Alcázars were built by the Moors upon Roman or Visigoth ruins that were greatly expanded by the Christians after the Reconquest. Among the most famous are found in Seville, Jeréz de la Frontera, Toledo, and Segovia. Some say that Walt Disney may have based the design of his magical castle of "Snow White and the Seven Dwarfs" on the alcázar in Segovia that sits high upon a rocky cliff 200 feet above the town.

Others insist that Disney's inspiration may have come from a particular castle in Germany or, most likely, a combination of different fairy-tale like castles he admired throughout Europe.

Alcázar in Segovia

Segovia, in central Spain, was a significant fortress town under the rule of Abd al-Rahman III. It also famous for its magnificent Roman aqueduct built during the time of Emperor Trajan in the first century AD, standing over 93 feet high that holds a dark legend.

The story begins with a young servant girl who grew weary and began complaining about her arduous daily trips to the springs in the valley below to fetch and carry water back home. In desperation, she made a pact with the devil and agreed to sell her soul if he could make the water reach her house before the sun rose the next morning. As the night progressed, she became frightened and began regretting her pact — even as the aqueduct was being formed to supply water to the city.

The young girl prayed for an early sunrise in order to beat the devil at his game and by the time the first ray of the sun appeared, there was but one stone left out of place. Her prayers were answered as this tremendous task was not completed in time and the devil did not get to possess the maiden's soul. To this day the aqueduct is also called Puente del Diablo (Devil's Bridge). Curiously, the 200,000 granite blocks that were used in its construction are held together by nothing more than force and gravity.

Alfama: The name of this ancient Moorish district in Lisbon comes from *al-hammah*, meaning "the baths" or "the fountains." Alfama is regarded as one of the oldest quarters in Lisbon as well as being the heart of historic Portugal.

Algarve: The name of this province in Portugal derives its name from *al-gharb*, "the west" as it is west of Spain. This town has a magnificent Atlantic coastal strip with fabulous beaches, cliffs, and sandstone rocks.

Algecíras (Al-heh-thee-ras): This southern town of Spain in the province of Cádiz derives its name from *al-jazirah*, "the peninsula" or "the island." Its original name is *al-Jazirah al-Khadra*, meaning "The green island." Algecíras was the gateway to al-Andalus from Africa and the first Spanish town captured by the Moors in 711.

Alhóndiga: Also pronounced *Alfóndiga*, this term designates an urban establishment such as an inn, where out of town merchants lodged with their goods and commercial transactions took place. It is derived from *al-funduq*, "the hotel." The *Corral de Carbon* in Granada is the only remaining intact alhóndiga that has survived in Spain.

Alicante (Alee-can-teh): This popular seaside tourist resort, situated on the eastern coast of Spain of the Costa Blanca, was first named *Akra Leuka*, meaning "white peak" or "bright hill" during the Greek/Carthaginian period when Carthaginian general, Hamilcar Barca, established a fortified settlement here. During the Roman era it was named *Lucentum*, meaning "city of light" or "bright city." The reasoning behind this is that Alicante has always displayed exceptionally luminous skies. When the Arabs arrived, the renamed it *Madinat al-Laqant*, or "city of Lucentum."

Port of Algecíras in Cádiz

Today, one can admire the impressive Moorish fortress known as Castillo de Santa Bárbara on the slopes of Mount Benacantil. Considered one of the largest of its kind in Europe, the castle was taken by King Alfonso X "El Sabio" or "The Wise" in 1248 on December 4, otherwise known as Saint Barbara's Day. Remains as far back as the Bronze Age have been discovered on this site.

Aljama: This is derived from *al-jama*, "the assembly" or "the congregation." The Arabs applied this term to Jewish and Mudéjar communities within their territories as well as to their larger mosques, such as the *La Mezquita Aljama de Córdoba*.

Aljibe (Al-hee-beh): This is derived from *al-jubb*, "the cistern" or "the reservoir." Aljibes were subterranean chambers or wells used for collecting, storing and distributing the town's water supply through channels and fountains. However another version is that it is derived from *al-hawd*, "the pond" or "the pool."

Entrance to the Castillo Santa Bárbara in Alicante

Almería: The name of this province where my grandfather was born is derived from *al-mariyah*, "the mirror," for the reflection of North Africa that is captured by the still Mediterranean waters. Or, according to other sources, it may derive from *al-meriya*, "the watchtower," in reference to the magnificent Moorish castle that once stood in Almería as the biggest in all of Europe.

Alminar: The name for the tower of the Mosque is derived from *al-menara* or "the minaret." It is also known in Castilian as *minarete*.

Almocabar: The name of the well-preserved 13th century gate found in the southern part of the Medina in Ronda is derived from *al-maqabir* that means "the cemetery." The reason behind this is that the Puerta Almocabar is located near the main cemetery that was situated outside the city walls as was the tradition by the Arabs. The Almocabar Gate served as one of the main entrances to the old Medina.

Almohades: This term comes from *al-muwahhid*, "the unitarian" or "he who affirms the unity of one God." This Berber dynasty ruled in al-Andalus and much of western North Africa during the 12th and 13th centuries.

Almorávides: This is the name of another Berber religious movement that ruled prior to the Almohads during the 11th and 12th centuries. Often referred to as a fanatical group from the Sahara, their name is derived from *al-mu-rabitun*, meaning "The people of the Ribat." The singular form is *al-murabit* and it may also be translated as "the monk warrior," as these people fiercely defended their faith.

4th Century BCE Punic-Roman Salting Pits at the foot of the Castle in Almuñecar

Almotacén (Almota-then): This is derived from *al-muhtásib*, "the overseer" or the government appointed official and inspector who oversaw the operations at the souks, or markets, making sure all functioned properly. He was also known as *as-sahib as-sûq*, roughly translated as "the officer of the zoco."

Almuñécar: This quaint town in the province of Granada derives its name from *al-munakkab*, meaning "the fortified town." Almuñécar has been a fishing village since 3,000 years ago when the Phoenicians knew it as *Sexi Firmum Julium*. The Romans gave to Almuñécar an aqueduct and the *Cueva de los Siete Palacios* (Cave of the Seven Palaces) that today houses a small archaeological museum. Among the many treasures on display is an ancient Egyptian vase dating to the 17th century BCE, as its inscription reveals. This is regarded as one of the oldest samples of writing to have been discovered in Spain. Its discovery this far from home can only be explained by the sacking of Egyptian tombs and the smuggling of treasures into Spain.

Almuñécar was considered one of the most important fish salting centers in the Mediterranean region going back to 5th century BCE or earlier. Remains have been excavated of a lucrative fish-salting industry that was begun by the Phoenicians and greatly expanded by the Romans, and to a lesser extent were also used by the Moors. These preserving salting pits, with narrow fresh water channels running in between, are known as *Salazónes*. Salazónes were also located in Almería, Málaga, Cádiz, and Cartagena.

The town where Abd al-Rahman I disembarked in 755 and founded al-Andalus is dotted with many watchtowers along the splendid and unblemished coastline. *Castillo de San Miguel*, which crowns the city, was originally built by the Romans during the first century BCE and later expanded by the Moors. Legend has it that it was here where the kings of Granada stored their riches. During the time of the Nasrid dynasty, the castle served as a summer retreat for the sultans; however, the dungeons were also home to political prisoners. Once Almuñécar fell to the Christians, the castle was named after the town's new patron saint, *San Miguel* or St. Michael. Gorgeous views of the town and the sea can be taken in from the castle's remains. Almuñécar was the last town to fall, in 1489, before the entire kingdom of Granada and Moorish Spain fell in 1492.

Presently, it is a little-known sub-tropical tourist resort unspoiled by commercialism and frequented mainly by German tourists. What I particularly remember about this town is the distinct scent of jasmine that constantly emanated from the gardens of the homes by the Mediterranean as I strolled by at sunset. Almuñécar is recognized as the tourist capital of the *Costa Tropical* (Tropical Coast) of Spain that also includes two major resort towns of Salobreña and Motril.

Alpujarra/Alpujarras: The name of this region and mountain range in Andalusia may be derived from *al-buheyra*, or "the lake." Through the center of the Alpujarra flows the *Guadalfeo River* that divides the region. The name of this river may come from *wadj* (river or valley) and *fiadan* (flood), as in "flooded river" or "flooded valley." This region remains green throughout the year due to the efficient irrigation methods that the Moors introduced long ago that are still in use today by the local farmers. Another likely theory is that this name is derived from *al-busherat*, meaning "the grasslands."

The extensive Alpujarra region encompasses parts of the provinces of Granada and Almería. Many Moriscos left Granada after the Reconquest and found refuge here by settling in the various villages of the Alpujarra region for about a century. Here lived the last Moorish king Boabdil for several months before retreating to Morocco. Traces of Moorish culture remain throughout the Alpujarra region, particularly in the traditional Berber-style residential architecture.

Ampurias: This town in the northeastern Catalonia region was founded by the Greeks around 600 BCE and later became a thriving Roman colony known as *Emporiae*. Its name is derived from the Greek *emporium*, "market place" or "commercial center," as it was located at the intersection of several commercial trade routes. The archaeological sites of the Greco-Roman ruins in this town are quite spectacular.

Andalucía (Andaloo-thee-a). The Vandals invaded southern Spain in 409 and it is generally believed that they named it *Vandalusia* or *Vandalicia* meaning "Land of the Vandals." The Arabs borrowed the Visigoth name and modified it into *Jazirat al-Andalus*, meaning "Peninsula of al-Andalus" or "Island of al-Andalus." The name was assigned exclusively to all the territories that were under Muslim control (including in Portugal) and not the entire Iberian Peninsula itself.

The first appearance of the name "al-Andalus" manifested in the form of a *dinar* dated to the year 716. This bilingual coin has "al-Andalus" on one side and the Latin "Spania" inscribed on the other.

The Vandals brought so much destruction and disruption wherever they settled that their name is almost the only trace they left in Spain. Could it be that the Moors kept the name as a reminder of their successful conquest and acquisition? So ruthless and barbaric were the Vandals that the word "vandalism" is traced back to them.

Many dismiss this theory and propose that Jazirat al-Andalus means "Island of the Atlantis" or "Island of the Atlantic," as Atlantis was believed to be situated between Spain and Northern Africa. There is a more recent theory of the origin of the name that seems more plausible. Researchers now suggest that it is an Arabic version of the Visigoth name of their kingdom, "*Landa-hlauts*," meaning "Land of raffles" or "Land of lotteries," as they divided and distributed their conquered lands according to their Germanic traditions through draws or raffles; a form of modern-day lottery. The Gothic term "hlauts" means "allotment" or "draw" and in old German it became "hlôz." This evolved into "los" in modern German and "lot" in French. Here lies the origin of the words "lottery," "lotería" in Spanish, and "loterie" in French. Around 716 the Moors likely began pronouncing it *Landalos*, which was soon understood as al-Andalus.

It wasn't until the 13th century that the Christian population began to refer to southern Spain as *Andalucía*. The natives were called *Andaluces* and so they have been ever since. A male is known as an *Andaluz* and a female as an *Andaluza*; however when reference is made to one from the past in al-Andalus, he or she is known as an Andalusí (plural *Andalusíes*). Andalusians, as they are known in English, are described by George Borrow as "living under the most glorious sun and benign heaven in Europe."

Arrabal: This term for a suburb situated on the outskirts of the city or Medina comes from *ar-rabad*, "the neighborhood" or "suburb." As recent as the summer of 2006, the ruins of an Arrabal called *al-Tabannin* (dated to the 11th century) were discovered and excavated in the center of Málaga, buried 2.20 meters in depth.

Axarquia: The name of this sub-tropical region in Andalusia comes from the Arabic *as-sharqiyya*, meaning "the east," as it is situated in the eastern region of the province of Málaga. This region on the Costa del Sol lies within the eastern third of the province of Málaga and includes the popular sea side resorts of Nerja, Torre del Mar, and Torrox.

Azahar (Athar): The Castilian word for "orange blossom" is derived from *az-zahr*, meaning "a flower."

Azulejos (Athu-leh-hos): The Castilian word for "tiles" comes from *az-zu-layj*, meaning "polished stone" or "glazed tile." Southern Spain became famous for its painted ceramic tiles and these ornaments often adorned the architecture and houses of Moorish Spain and Portugal. Azulejos could be decorated or plain and were used to protect and beautify the floors and walls. The first samples used in architecture are believed to be dated to the late 12th century. Triana, the former Gypsy neighborhood of Seville then known as *Taryana*, was renowned for its production of such glazed tiles. It is interesting to note that these tiles often come in blue and the Spanish word for this color is *azul*. A wonderful example is the 20th century Plaza de España in Seville with its blue-tiled alcoves that honor each of the provinces of Spain.

Badajoz (Badahoth) is situated on the western side of Spain and close to the Portuguese border. *Batalyaws*, as this town was known to the Moors, was the capital of a small Moorish Taifa kingdom after the fall of the Caliphate in the 11th century. Its Arabic name is believed to have derived from the Roman name for this town, *Pax Augusta*. The letter "p" does not exist in the Arabic language and has always been substituted with a "b."

Baeza (Baetha): There is documented proof that this town in Jaén existed during Roman rule and was known as *Beatia* or *Vivatia*. During Visigoth rule it was a prosperous city. Under the Moors it was known as *al-Bayyasa* and it became the first town to be conquered by the Catholic rulers during the 13ᵗʰ century.

Barrio: This word meaning "neighborhood" or "suburb" is derived from *barrî*, meaning "outside," as these regions were outside the city proper.

Benalmádena: The name of this beach resort town in the province of Málaga is derived from *ibn al-ma'din,* meaning "sons of the mines," as several valuable mines existed in this area. It is also possible that the Arabic name translates as "sons or descendants of the Madina family." Another theory is that it is derived from ibn al-Madinat or "sons or descendants of the city." In Castilian, it evolved into *Benalmaina* and then into its present form. Benalmádena is now a popular resort for British tourists and residents and one of the most visited areas in Spain.

The town's lack of historical architecture is recompensed by the charm of its present-day features. The lovely *Castillo Bil- Bil* was built in 1934 in the center of town by the sea. The building was designed in a classic red-tiled Moroccan style that houses such cultural events as concerts, conferences, exhibitions, and formal social events.

The Neo-Arabic Bil-Bil Castle on the coast of Benalmádena

Berebere: This one is not, in fact, an Arabism; the Spanish word for "Berber" is derived from the Latin *barbarus* that translates into "outsiders." It was the Romans who coined this term for the ancestors of today's Tunisians, who are now known as *Imazighen*.

On one of my trips to Andalusia, I took the ferry from Algeciras to Ceuta for the purpose of visiting Tangier, a place special to me as this is where my grandparents lived, met, and married about a century ago. Walking through the clothes and linen market of Tetuan with my small tour group, I admired the thick fabrics of vivid colors that the women use for home decoration as well as for clothing. Then suddenly and much to my surprise, a Berber sales-woman put her hands firmly upon my shoulders, to which my tour guide Muhammad quickly gave me a reassuring wink and nod of approval. The Berber woman was very friendly as she continuously smiled but never ut-tered a single word. She motioned me to remain still and stretch my arms out to the sides as she proceeded to select pieces of fabric from her table. She began dressing me over my clothes, using four different pieces of fabric. The first piece she fastened as a strapless tunic under my arms; the second was wrapped as a shawl over my shoulders; the third was draped across my face and the final piece crowned my head holding the face veil in place. In less than five minutes, I was transformed into a Berber woman!

The author and tour guide in Tetuan, Morocco

Cádiz (Ka-deeth): The Phoenicians originally named this town *Gadir*, meaning "fortified city." To this day, citizens of this province are still known as *Gaditanos*. This town was later known as *Gaderia* by the Greeks and *Gades* by the Romans. Its present name is derived from the Moors who pronounced it as *Qádis*.

Calahorra: The name of this defense tower in Córdoba is said to have come from *Qalat al-Harrah*, "fortress of freedom." *Qalat* is another term for "castle," as is *Qasar*. However, the hill town of Calahorra, in Northern Spain on the right bank of the Ebro River and one of the oldest in the peninsula, was known as *Calagurris* in pre-Roman times and that suggests an older origin for this name.

Today the Tower of Calahorra houses a small museum called *Vivo de Al-Andalus* that is well worth visiting. Inside are artifacts and miniature exhibits of the many accomplishments and aspects of life in Moorish Córdoba under the three faiths. Arab-Andalusí music, modern technology, and audio visual tools skillfully evoke the ambiance and essence of life in Córdoba during its Golden Age.

Calderería: This is the name of the two narrow and steep streets that run perpendicular to each other in the lower Albayzín area of Granada that form a most charming Arabic bazaar. The name Calderería comes from *kelderara*, meaning "cauldron-makers" or "pot makers," after the crafts workshops that have been here for centuries. Both Calderería Nueva (new) and Calderería Vieja (old) are filled with Moroccan souvenir shops and dozens of *teterías* (tea houses). *Tetería Kasbah* on Calderería Nueva where they serve a delicious menu of Moroccan delights with Oriental dancers performing is well worth visiting.

Califa: This title is derived from *Jalifah* or *Khalifa*, meaning "Successor" as in "to Muhammad." The Caliph functioned as the religious and political leader of Islamic people whose duties included exercising civil and spiritual power in the name of Muhammad. During the 10th century, Abd al-Rahman III proclaimed full independence of the emirate that had been established by Abd al-Rahman I two centuries earlier by becoming the first Caliph of al-Andalus.

Cármenes: This word is derived from *karm*, "garden" or "vineyard." As Córdoba is known as the *Ciudad de los Patios* (City of Patios), Granada is known as the *Ciudad de los Cármenes* that are typical of this town.

Cármen of Flemish artist Max Moreau (1902-1992) with views to the Alhambra that has been converted into a museum and art gallery

Cartagena (Carta-hena): This town in the province of Murcia was founded circa 230 BCE as *Qart Hadast*, translating in Punic as "new city." Cartagena, on the south eastern coast, was established as the capital in 223 BCE and the Romans renamed it *Carthago Nova* or "New Carthage." This town became the capital of Byzantine Emperor Justinian in c. 554. The Moors, who knew it as *Qartachana*, arrived and conquered the region in 734 until it fell to the Christians in 1254.

Ceuta (Theh-oota): This is an autonomous community of Spain situated on the northern tip of Morocco. In Arabic it is known as *Sabta or Sebta*, a name believed to come from the Roman name of this port city *Septem*, meaning "seven" in reference to the nearby seven hills. Prior to the Statute of Autonomy in 1995, Ceuta was partly administered by the province of Cádiz.

The other Spanish enclave in Morocco is *Melilla*, known in Arabic as *Melilia*. Melilla was captured by the Spaniards in the fall of 1497, just five years after they had taken possession of Granada. Melilla still remains a Spanish outpost on the coast of Morocco and like Ceuta, is recognized as part of the country by the Spanish Government. Although it is often referred to being administered by the province of Málaga, the General Directorate of Public Administration of the Autonomous City of Melilla informed me that "Melilla has never at any moment in time ever belonged to Málaga or any other province in Andalusia. However, certain judicial matters are handled by the Autonomous Community of Andalusia."

Córdoba: The name of this province comes from the Punic *Qart Tuba*, meaning "city of Ba'al." The ancient Semitic worship of the cult of Ba'al (also known as *Tuba*) goes as far back as 14th century BCE. The Romans knew it as *Carta Tuba* or "city of Tuba," which became *Córduba*, and the Moors pronounced it *Qurtuba* that evolved into *Córdova* and into its present form.

Dinero: This Castilian word for "money" is derived from the Arab *dinars* or coins that were familiar in al-Andalus. This in turn evolved from the name of the small Roman silver coins known as *denarii*.

El Cid: The name of the legendary Spanish warrior and hero of the 11th century is derived from the Arabic honorific title *Sayyid* or *as-Sid*, meaning "The Lord" or "Sir," that today survives in the form of *Sidi*. A monument of El Cid "El Campeador" (The Champion), the hero riding on horseback, is found in Seville.

Emir: This political title comes from *Amr*, meaning "Ruler" or "Prince." The Emir was one of the first governors that ruled al-Andalus but remained dependent upon the Caliphate of Damascus.

España: There are several theories to the origins of this name. In the ancient Basque language, *ezpaña* means "extremity" or "shoulder" and Spain certainly does form the southwestern "extremity" of continental Europe. Interestingly, the Basque word *ezpain* is translated as "border," "edge," or "rim."

When the Phoenicians and Carthaginians arrived, they called the Iberian Peninsula *Span* or *Spania*. This is said to mean "hidden land" — or possibly even "land of the rabbit," as they apparently discovered the land to be plentiful with this animal which in Punic was called *Tsepan*.

When the Romans conquered the land, it became *Hispania*, which the Moors later pronounced as *Ishbaniya*, replacing the letter "p" with a "b" as is customary in Arabic. This was the name by which the Moors used to refer to the small northern areas in the mountains of Asturias and the Cantabrian coast that they were unable to possess.

The Clock Tower in Estepona

Este-pona: The name of this peaceful sea-side town in Málaga at the foot of the Sierra Bermeja is derived from the Arabic *Estebbuna*, as it was so named by the Moors. In Estepona lie the ruins of a once im-portant Ara-bic fortress dated to the 9th century named *El Castillo del Nicio*. The history of this town goes as far back as the Phoenicians who settled here. However, ancient remains have been found in Estepona that are dated as far back as the Neolithic Age. Several archaeological sites dated to the Phoenician and Roman Period are also found that may have been part of the important ancient Roman city of *Salduba* (Marbella) near the *Guadalmansa* River.

The Tower of the parish church of La Virgen de los Remedios

During Roman times, Estepona was known as *Cilniana*. Seven watchtowers or *Torres Almenaras* of Phoenician and Roman origin, greatly enlarged and restored by the Arabs, dot the 13-mile coastline of Estepona. The *Torre del Reloj* or Clock Tower is another gift from the Moors that was once the minaret of the local mosque. Once the town was conquered by the Catholic Kings during the late 15th century, the mosque was converted into a church and the minaret was used as a bell tower. The Clock Tower is considered the oldest building in the Costa del Sol.

Another curious site is the tower of the church known *Virgen de los Remedios* (Our Lady of Redemption) that was built during the 18th century. The church was once used as a Franciscan Monastery. The tower can be seen rising above the buildings as it stands out when viewed from various vantage points throughout the town.

Flamenco: Not only are the origins of Flamenco often disputed but so is the etymology of its name. Many theories have developed over the years and, like the name "Andalusia," is still open to debate. According to documented evidence, "Flamenco" did not become a synonym for Andalusian Gypsies and the class of Spaniards who either associated with them or led a similar lifestyle until the late 18ᵗʰ century. At this time, "Flamenco" was a derogatory term describing one who was arrogant, defiant, proud, ostentatious, flamboyant, flirtatious, over-confident, and flashy.

One of the two most widely accepted theories of the word "Flamenco" is that it derives from the colloquial Arabic term *Fellah al-Mengu*, roughly translating as "fugitive peasants" or "wandering country folk." After the Reconquest, the Moriscos united with, yet differentiated themselves from, the wandering Gypsies and may have referred to the Gypsies in this manner. Another theory is that it may be related to *Flahencu*, a term used to refer to Morisco songs from the Alpujarra region. It may have also derived from *Felahikum*, meaning "the farmer" or "countryman."

The most credible theory is based on the fact that "Flamenco" is the Spanish word for a Flemish native or one from Flanders. The grandson of Catholic Monarchs, King Fernando and Queen Isabella, was born in Flanders (Netherlands) in 1500 to a Spanish mother (*Juana La Loca* or "Joan the Mad") and a Habsburg father (*Felipe el Hermoso* or "Philippe the Handsome"). Being the only heir to the throne, the young boy inherited the land of Spain and during the early 16ᵗʰ century, Emperor Charles V of Flanders also became King Carlos I of Spain.

Being brought up in Flanders, Carlos I and his Flemish courtiers and soldiers spoke little Spanish and so became known as Flamencos, or "the Flemish." In Spain, they were resented as they were considered "foreigners" who had invaded their territory and did not care to learn the language nor to show any interest in any cultural aspect of Spain whatsoever. The Flamencos quickly attracted attention to themselves with their flashy and colorful garments. The Flemish were regarded by the Spaniards as boisterous, haughty, and dashing men of style, pride, and self-confidence; traits the locals believed were somewhat shared with the character of the Gypsy. The term soon came to describe uncouth or unrefined behavior. The term eventually came to encompass all foreigners living in Andalusia.

Another theory is that the term "Flamenco" was given to the many Gypsies that passed through Flanders before they actually arrived in Spain. The Flemish singers from the choir of the Court of Carlos I were recognized for their solemn style of singing and eventually the connection between one from Flanders (Flamenco) and a singer (Gypsy) became synonymous. Yet another related theory is that the Flemish noblemen often spent time with the Gypsies for entertainment and amusement purposes and the name may have eventually transferred to the Gypsies by association through this avenue.

The Gypsies came to be known as Flamencos during the late 1700s as well as their music, song and dance. As the art form grew in popularity, its derogatory meaning began to dissipate and the term became acceptable as a synonym for "Gitano." By the middle of the 19th century the term was applied to the music of the Spanish Gypsies or Gitanos who performed in the Café Cantantes. It was at this point that the rules and structure of classical Flamenco tradition were established.

The relation between "Flamenco" and "flame" is another, albeit less plausible, theory of the origins of the name based upon the "fiery" essence of Flamenco.

Another theory (with few supporters) is that the word Flamenco was originally the name of a knife. This appears in a one-act comedy written during the 18th century by *González Del Castillo* where reference is made to "Flamenco" as a knife or dagger.

Still others propose that the name has Jewish roots. Jews who left Spain rather than choosing conversion were permitted their solemn, religious songs in Flanders without oppression. Those who remained referred to these chants as "Flamenco," or "from Flanders." Some also claim that the Flamenco term "*jaleo*" comes from *jalel*, the Hebrew word for "encourage," as in the encouragement given to an artist while performing. However, other sources indicate the origins of "jaleo" to be Arabic, from *hallala*, meaning "noisy cheer."

Perhaps the most unlikely theory is that the word evolved from the same word in Spanish for a flamingo bird. This flimsy link recognizes the fact that this elegant bird stands tall and proud and makes a move similar to one of the Flamenco dancer's poses, with comparable postures such as gracefully holding the head up high and rhythmically turning the head from side to side, while stomping the ground. The word "flamingo" itself is related to the Latin *flamma*, "flame," as the plumage of this bird can be fiery red.

Today, the term is used as a colloquial adjective. When someone is described or accused of "being flamenco" or "flamenco," a cocky, haughty, stubborn, or self-righteous attitude is implied. It does not describe the given nature of person but a temporary state of being.

Fuengirola (Fuen-hee-rola) This is a charming seaside town in the province of Málaga that was first colonized by the Phoenicians, who named it *Suel*. The Arabs named it *Sohail* or *Suhayl* and legend has it that its name is derived from a star that could only be seen from the town's landmark, the ancient hilltop castle named *Castillo Sohail.*

Castillo Sohail in Fuengirola

Originally an Ibero-Carthaginian settlement, Fuengirola was later to be inhabited by Romans and then the Moors. First documented during the 7th century BCE, the castle was built upon a small hill overlooking the Mediterranean Sea in order to protect against pirates. Abd al-Rahman III ordered its reconstruction as a fortress during the mid 10th century. The coastal castle and fortress were destroyed during the late 15th century and rebuilt once again during the 18th century. During the Reconquest the town's name was radically altered to *Font Jirola*, apparently after a fountain that flowed or spring that emerged from the foot of Castillo Sohail. Another theory is that its name is derived from the instruments known as "girolas" that the fishermen used in their trade, or, more likely, the name comes from "girola" which is the Castilian term for an ambulatory; the covered passageways inside a cathedral or monastery around the area also known as the cloister.

Staircase at Gibralfaro Castle in Málaga

Generalife (Hen-era-lee-feh): The name of the summer palace of the Alhambra is derived from *Ganna al–Arif*, meaning "garden of the architect." The architect in question is believed to be Allah, as these gardens simulate paradise on earth and were created in honor of the "architect" of the universe.

Gibralfaro: This 14th century fortress in Málaga derives its name from *Gebel Faro*, meaning "lighthouse hill" or "lighthouse mountain"; "faro" in turn comes from the Greek *faruh*, meaning "lighthouse."

Gibraltar: As mentioned earlier, this name is derived from *Gebel al-Tariq*, meaning "hill of Tariq" or "Tariq's mountain," named after Tariq ibn Ziyad, who began his campaign here in 711.

The Rock of Gibraltar

The most impressive site is the "Tower of Homage" built during the 14th century over the ruins of an 8th and 11th century Moorish castle — it is currently housing a short-term prison.

Tower of Homage at Gibraltar

Conquered by the Christians in 1212, Gibraltar was seized by British naval forces in 1704. Spain eventually ceded the territory to Britain in 1713, with the Treaty of Utrecht — a highly sensitive issue to many Spaniards to this day.

The Upper Rock is home to the only wild monkeys in Europe, the famous Barbary Macaques that roam freely about. A popular belief suggests that Gibraltar will remain British as long as this species lives on the Rock. When the monkey population was drastically dwindling during World War II, Winston Churchill gave the order to replenish them.

Barbary Macaques upon a car rooftop at the Upper Rock of Gibraltar

Gitano/Gitana (Hee-tano/Hee-tana): The origin of this term is Castilian. The Gypsies who migrated to Spain from, it is said, northern India, during the 15th century claimed to be of royal lineage from a place called the Kingdom of Little Egypt, an area intimated to have included southern Greece and western Turkey. These tribes or families with their Dukes, Counts, and Earls, brought with them a document bearing the protection and signature of Emperor Sigismund who was King of Hungary and Bohemia as well as Holy Emperor of Rome and Germany, declaring that these people originated from Little Egypt. It was by these means that they began to be known as "The Egyptians." True Egyptians were called *Egiptanos* and Gypsies became known by the abbreviated form, *Gitanos*. Nowadays, in English it is considered polite to call them *Rom* or *Roma*, rather than Gypsies. In Spain they are still known as Gitanos and natives from Egypt are called Egipcios.

Granada: Granada was known as *Ilbyr* by the Iberians and *Ildurir* or *Ilturir* by the time the Greeks arrived during the 8th century BCE. By the 5th century BCE, the Greeks had established a colony in this region named *Elybirge*. The Romans renamed it *Ilbira* or *Iliibris* and the Visigoths knew it as *Eliberri*. Under the Moors, this region was known as *Medina Elvira* at least until the 10th century, and was the foundation of the city of Granada that we know today. Medina Elvira was destroyed in 1010 and was reborn as the independent kingdom of *Madinat Gharnatah* in 1013.

The oldest hypothesis is that the city derived its name from the daughter of Hercules, who was named *Granata*. A more probable theory is that it is derived from the name of the old Jewish ghetto named *Gharnatah*. By the time the Moors arrived, a large Jewish community was already established on the left bank of the Darro River in central Granada. The Moors re-named it *Gharnatah al-Yahud*, or "Granada of the Jews." Little is known about this ancient Jewish quarter, now called the *Realejo*; however a mention in 4th century documents of the Council of Elvira reveals its considerable relevance.

The province's name is said to bear no relation to the pomegranate known in Spanish as a *granada*. Interestingly, its botanical term is *punica granatum*, referring to the Phoenicians who were active in spreading its cultivation here thousands of years ago.

Guadalquivír: The name is derived from *al-Wadj al-Kabir*, "the big river" or "the great river." The Guadalquivír is one of Spain's five great rivers and it flows from east to west across central Andalusia into the Atlantic Ocean. During Roman times the Guadalquivir River was known as *Baetis*.

Guitarra: This is derived from *Quitara*, which in turn comes from the Latin *Cithara*, that itself is derived from the Greek name for the musical instrument known as *Kithara*.

Harén: The Castilian word for "harem" comes from the Arabic *haram*, meaning "forbidden" or "prohibited." Webster's Encyclopedia defines a harem as "a Mohammedan house in which women are secluded."

Huelva (Wel-vah): The Phoenicians named this town *Onos Baal*, meaning "fortress of Ba'al" in honor of their god. The Romans pronounced it as *Onuba* and the Moors re-named it *Walbah* or *Guelbah*.

Iberia: Spain's original name was *Iberia* and its people were *Iberians*, a name bestowed upon by the ancient Greeks later in history after the *Iber* or *Iberus* River. Known as the *Rio Ebro* in Spanish, this is one of the country's great five rivers that flows eastward to the Mediterranean Sea. The name "Iberus" may come from the Basque word *ibar* ("valley," "lowlands" or "river-bank"). It is also worth mentioning that *ibai* is the Basque word for "river."

Jaén (Ha-en) This town was known as *Auringis* or *Aurgi* by the Romans circa 207 BCE and later was renamed *Geén* when it was conquered by the Moors in 712. The Arabic name translates to "caravan route" or "crossroads of caravans," as significant trading roads converged here rendering it an important hub within the main routes that connected various towns during Moorish rule. During the 9th century it became known as *Geen* or *Yayyan* (pronounced as *Jayan*), possibly meaning "area of an abundance of water." When it passed onto Christians hands in 1246 it became known as *Xauen* (pronounced as *Zawen*), which some say means "sanctuary."

Jeréz de la Frontera (He-reth): This town was known as *Asta Regia* under the Romans. The Moors named this town *Shareesh*, which evolved into *Xeres* in Old Castilian, from which its present form is derived. The second half of the name is due to the fact that it was a "frontier" town situated between what was once Moorish and Christian territory. The fortified Moorish town was ultimately conquered by the Christians in 1264.

Jeréz de la Frontera has been celebrated for its wine production for over 3,000 years. It was the British who were fond of a particular Spanish type of wine that they named "sherry" after the Arabic name for this region in Cádiz where it was and still is produced. Sherry was consumed by the Moors for medicinal purposes and was exported to England possibly as far back as the 13th century.

Laúd: The Spanish word for "lute" is derived from *al-ud*, meaning "of wood," the material used in its construction.

Lisboa: The capital of Portugal was founded by the Phoenicians as *Alisi-bbo* or *Alis Ubbo*, meaning "good harbor." The Greeks knew it as *Olissipo*; similar sounding, yet may be derived from "Ulysses" who many believe was the founder of the city. The Romans pronounced it *Olissipona* and later, *Lissapona*. When the Moors conquered the land they pronounced it *al-Oshbuna*, evolving into *Lashbuna* and into its present form. Lisbon was conquered by the Moors in 711 and remained in their hands until 1147, when it was conquered by the Christians.

Loja: The birth town of renowned writer and physician *Ibn al-Khatib* was known as *Madinat Lawsa*, from where its present name is derived. Located about 35 miles west of Granada, in the heart of Andalusia, Loja is known for the abundance of springs that supply fountains adorning this town, including the *Fuente de la Mora*, or the "Fountain of the Moorish Maiden," with its 25 spouts. Loja was captured by the Christians in 1486 but traces of its Moorish heritage remain in the quarter of the Alcazába.

Madrid (Madreeth): The author's birthplace was founded by the Moors during the 9th century. They named it Madinat Majerit, meaning "city of a soft and fresh breeze." In 1623, Céspedes and Meneses wrote:

> Los Moros...la dieron nuevo nombre, y el mismo que hoy conserva, aludiendo la significación del a una de sus mayores excelencias, a sus frescos y saludables aires, porque Madrid no otra cosa significa en su lengua que lugar de buenos aires: y esto es tan cierto que ni en lo restante de España, ni aun de la mitad del Orbe, se conoce sitio mas sano.

> The Moors...bestowed this name upon her, the same that is in use today, alluding to the significance of one of her finest qualities, her fresh and inviting breezes, because Madrid in this language means nothing other than a place of fine breezes: and this is for sure, as no more salubrious spot can be found, not in the rest of Spain, nor anywhere else on the globe.

Another theory is that the name comes from the Arabic term *majrá*, or *matrice*, in Latin. To "Majrá" was added the suffix "it" and the name became Majerit, meaning "source of water" or "place of abundant waters," referring to the numerous *qanat* or underground irrigation canals and ditches constructed by the Moors to raise water throughout al-Andalus and Madrid (or *Madrí*, as it is often pronounced). "Majerit" may also have referred to the local River Manzanares, the town's source of water. Others believe that that the city's name is derived from its Roman name of *Miacum*, that evolved into *Maioritum*.

The first fortress in Majerit was built under the order of Emir Muhammad I (852-886), from Córdoba, son of Abderahman II; thus he founded the city. The site of this fortress is where the Royal Palace stands today. However, it was not until the late 10th century that it is mentioned in chronicles. During the 11th century Madrid belonged to the kingdom of the Taifa of Toledo; it became a major cause of disputes between the Arabs and Christians until it was conquered by Alfonso VI two centuries later, in 1085. During the 16th century, it was designated the country's capital and has remained such ever since.

Málaga: It was the Phoenicians would first settled here, followed by the Greeks, who founded *Mainake* about 26 kilometers to the east in 700 BC. Mainake became a significant center for trade under Roman rule, when it was known as *Menoba*. The name "Malaga" is derived from the Punic and Arabic word "*malac*," meaning "salt." The Romans named the town *Malaca*, and like with most ancient Andalusian cities, it began to flourish under their rule. Known as Malak*ah*, to the Moors, this town was an important settlement for the trade of salt fish.

Medina: This is derived from the Arabic *al-madinat*, meaning the "the city" or urban center of a Muslim town. A smaller city or *la almudena* is derived from the same source, albeit from the diminutive form, al-*mudayna* (little city).

Mezquita (Meth-keeta): The Spanish term for "mosque" comes from the Arabic *Masjid*, meaning "the place where one prostrates oneself."

Mojácar (Mo-Ha-ka): Mojácar is a quaint coastal town in the province of Almería. Its name is believed to be derived from the Arabic *Moxacar* or *Muxacra*, a corruption of the Latin *Musacra*, which comes from the Greeks/Phoenicians who arrived here circa 1100 BCE and named it *Murgis Akra*, meaning "upper city of Murgis" or "high point of Murgis." Philosopher, author, and Roman commander Pliny the Elder (23-79 AD) refers to *Murgis* as a "frontier town of Boetica" (Baética) in his "Third Book of the History of Nature." Another theory is that "Mojácar" is derived from the Latin *Mons Sacra* or "sacred mountain."

The old village or Old Mojácar is perched upon a hilltop facing the Mediterranean, overlooking miles of unblemished beaches. The town has been occupied by many inhabitants throughout history and today Mojácar remains culturally diversified as it is home to a large international blend of Europeans (mainly British) who have taken up residence here.

15th Century La Puerta de la Almedina in Mojácar

In the old village stands the only gate within the town, known as *La Puerta de la Almedina* (the door to the city), dated to the 15th century — according to the sign on the upper right. Until the middle of the 20th century, the women of Mojácar wore the *almalafa* or long veiled dress and were known as *las tapadas* or "the covered ones."

Moro: The Spanish translation for "Moor" is derived from the Latin *Mauri* or *Maurus*, the name of a Berber tribe from what was once the Roman province of Mauritania, on the Mediterranean coast of North Africa. Mauritania became part of the Roman Empire in 33 BCE and it incorporated northern Morocco and western Algeria; however, it is not the same region we call Mauritania today.

"El Moro" by Manuel Ruiz, 1961

The Romans referred to all non-Christian natives of North Africa as "Mauri" and that included all Arabs and Berbers who settled in Spain, as well as anyone with a dark complexion. The Spaniards used the term in a slightly derogatory manner, and the Moors never referred to themselves as such. Moroccans are known as *Marroquís*, and their native land as *Marruecos*.

Mozárabe (Mo-tharabe): This term is derived from *must'arab*, meaning "one who would be an Arab." It refers to a Spanish Christian who lived in al-Andalus under Muslim rule. The Mozárabes adopted certain aspects of Arab culture but were not Muslims, as they were permitted to practice their Catholic religion. It is also the name of a style of architecture developed by Christian refugees that fled Córdoba during the 9th and 10th centuries. This type of architecture can be found in the northern parts of Spain, particularly in Zaragoza, León, and Galicia.

Mudéjar (Mu-dehar): This term is derived from *mudaÿÿan* meaning "allowed to stay" or "domesticated." It pejoratively refers to a Muslim who did not convert but remained in Christian territories of Spain after the Reconquest. Interestingly, the Spanish word for "remain" or "stay" is *dejar*. Mudéjar also refers to the style of architecture developed by the Moors that was evident in Christian Spain between the 12th and 16th centuries. The Alcázar and La Giralda in Seville are among the finest examples of Mudéjar architecture.

Muladíes: This term is derived from *muwalladun*, meaning "converted family." This refers to Spanish Muslims and the descendants of Christians who converted to Islam. Muladíes were born Muslim as the offspring of mixed marriages between Muslims and Christians.

View from the Balcon de Europa in Nerja

Murcia (Moorthia): This town was officially founded in 825 by Abd al-Rahman II as *Medina Mursiya*, meaning "strong city" or "fortified city." Founded upon the site of a former Roman colony, Medina Mursiya was not completely established until 831. Situated in the southeast, Murcia has quaint villages where a great deal of Moorish influence can still be seen.

Nerja (Ner-ha): Nerja is located in the province of Málaga and was founded by Abd al-Rahman III during the 10th century. It was given the name of *Narixa*, derived from *narija*, or "abundant springs," for its fresh and flowing mountain water.

In Nerja you will find the *Balcon de Europa* (Balcony of Europe) with its breathtaking views of the Mediterranean stretching to North Africa. This title was bestowed upon it by the King Alfonso XIII (1886-1941) when he visited the spot.

This cliff-top viewing point overlooking the Mediterranean from the center of the town has a marble-paved and palm-tree-lined promenade that was built in 1487 along the edge of a cliff over a former 9th century Moorish castle. Nerja is a fashionable beach resort and picturesque village, best known for the prehistoric Paleolithic caves situated in the slopes of the Sierra Almijara Mountains a few miles from the city center. During the summer, Flamenco and classical concerts are held in a cavern that has been converted into a concert hall. Presently, only a third of the caves are open for tourists. The Caves of Nerja are regarded as "the natural cathedral of the Costa del Sol." As the holiday capital of the *Axarquia* region of Andalusia, Nerja has the best weather in this region and Axarquia is considered as having the best climate in Europe.

La Noria de la Albolafia in Córdoba

Noria: The Spanish word for "waterwheel" is derived from its Arabic name of *al-na'wra.* This was one of the many great gifts the Moors gave to Spain and it was indispensable in supplying water through channels to the mosque and Medina. An excellent example remains by the Roman Bridge on the Guadalquivír River in Córdoba, known as *La Noria de la Albolafia.*

This hydraulic wheel was built between 1131 and 1138 under the orders of the Almoravid governor of Córdoba. It was dismantled during the 15th century, as the noise it emitted prevented the Queen of Spain from getting a good night's sleep. This waterwheel was remodeled as a windmill during the 16ᵗʰ century and during the 20ᵗʰ century was subjected to less than adequate restorations.

Ojalá (O-ha-laah): This is an everyday expression that is derived from the equally popular Arabic saying, *Insha' Allah* meaning "I hope so," "God willing" or "Allah willing!" Another popular Spanish expression is *Albricias* derived from *al-bisharah*, meaning "thank God" or "Eureka!"

Olé: This popular cheer and expression of approval and encouragement is derived from the Muslim expression of *Allah* or *wa'Allah* (by Allah). It was modified, for shouting Allah's name was sure to bring serious repercussions during and after the Reconquest. It has a similar meaning as "Bravo!" and is often expressed at Flamenco shows and bullfights.

You will also often hear the word *ále*, an expression with a similar meaning as "well done" that is often shouted out at peak moments of a Flamenco performance to encourage the artist. It is also spoken in everyday conversations meaning "there you go" or "now you are fine." It actually sounds quite similar to the French *allez*, meaning "go," however the emphasis is placed here on the last syllable.

Another expression is *ála*, that is used after someone makes a remark that seems ridiculous, exaggerated, unbelievable, inappropriate, rude, or incompetent.

Pandereta: The Spanish word for "tambourine" comes from its Arabic name, *bandair*. This musical instrument of accompaniment was quite popular in the music and dances of Moorish Spain.

Portugal: This name is derived from the Latin *portus cale*, meaning "warm harbor." As in Spain, many towns in Portugal retain the Latin version of their Arabic names, such as Lisbon (al-Oshbuna) and Algarve (al-Gharb).

Ronda: Ronda is one of the oldest cities in Spain. Situated in northern Málaga, its slogan is *Ciudad Soñada* or "the Dream City." Its name derives from its Roman name of *Arunda*, as it was founded by the Roman general Scipio. The name of "Arunda" has been translated as "surrounded by mountains."

In the year 713 the small settlement was conquered by the Moors and became known as *Izna Rand Onda* meaning "the town of the fortress." It was named after the Moorish fort that was built upon the ruins of an earlier Roman castle known as *Castillo de Laurus*, built in 132 BC under the orders of Scipio. Ronda became an important settlement under the Moors and during the Taifa period, Izna Rand Onda became the capital of one of the Andalusí provinces or *Kura* known as *Takurunna*. By the late 9th century it was known as the walled city of *Madinat Runda*.

The Old Town quarter of Ronda

This town of spectacular scenery and unique beauty sits high in the Serranía de Ronda Mountains. Ronda is divided in half by the *El Tajo* gorge that plunges for 130 meters on three sides into Rio Guadelvín. It is crossed by three bridges: *Puente Romano* or *Puente San Miguel* from the 13th or 14th century; *Puente Viejo* (Old Bridge) or *Puente Arabe* from the 17th century; and *Puente Nuevo* (New Bridge) dated to the 18th century.

El Puente Arabe of the 17th century

Ronda has a distinctive Moorish quarter as well as excavated remains of Arab baths dated to the 13th century, when Ronda was the capital of a Taifa. These baths are among the best preserved in the country and they were in use until the beginning of the 17th century.

Ruins of the Arab Baths in Ronda

Ronda is also home to the oldest and largest bullring in the country, dated to 1785. The arena is open to visitors and houses a museum of Spain's finest bullfighters, or matadors. The first professional bullfighter is believed to have been Pedro Romero (1754-1839), born in Ronda. Legend has it that he slew his first bull at the age of 17 and throughout his lifetime killed 5,000 more.

Another important cultural site in Ronda is the magnificent early 14th century Mondragón Palace that, according to legend, was once the home of the King of Ronda, *Abb el Malik* or *Abomelic* in Castilian, who was the son of *Abul Hassan*, the Sultan of Morocco. The last Muslim governor, *Hamel el Zegrí*, also resided in this palace as did King Fernando and Queen Isabella during the late 15th century.

Ronda's unique remote scenery and hidden spots made it a hideout for Moriscos, and the storied *bandoleros* or bandits who rebelled against the Catholic Kings in 1501. Bandoleros were robbing wealthy tourists well into the 20th century. Some of these bandits have been elevated to legendary status and their history can be found at the *Museo Del Bandolero*, the only one of its kind in Spain, located in the heart of the city of Ronda.

White-washed houses overlooking El Tajo

Another monument worth seeing is the restored minaret of St. Sebastián. The *alminar* or minaret is all that remains of a mosque that was destroyed after the Reconquest. It formerly functioned as the small tower of an old mosque and later was incorporated into the church of San Sebastián as a bell tower. You can clearly make out the difference in architectural styles and time periods. The first two sections are of Muslim origin, built during the 14th century, with the traditional horseshoe arched doorway and windows, while the highest was built during the Christian period to house the belfry.

The Tower or Minaret of San Sebastián in the old Moorish quarter

La Puerta de Almocábar or the Almocabar Gate is well preserved and situated on the southern part of the Medina. Dated to the 13th century, it was greatly restored and altered in form three centuries later. The triple-arched

Gate was located near the main cemetery outside the city walls and served as the main entrance into the Medina.

13th Century Puerta de Almocábar

The walls of *La Xijara* or *Lacijara* in the east along with the Almocabar Gate in the south were built by *Abú-Nur*, who fortified and expanded much of the town during the 11th century. Located in the rocky plateau above the river Guadelvín, these walls formed a part of the heavy defense fortification of Moorish Ronda. The Puerta de La Xijara was formerly the entrance into the Jewish quarter.

Salobreña: The name of this resort town along the coast in the province of Granada was *Salambina* when it was occupied by the Carthaginians. The Romans renamed it *Segalvina* and the Moors pronounced it *Salawbiniya*. Salobreña was conquered by the Catholic Monarchs in 1489 and today it forms part of the Costa Tropical of Spain.

Sevilla (Sevi-ya): Founded by the Tartessians, Seville was conquered by Julius Caesar in 56 BCE and renamed *Hispalis*. The origin of this name is unknown; however, there is a theory presented by Saint Isidore of Seville (born in Cartagena during the 6th century), who compiled an encyclopedia of etymologies known as *Etymologiae*. He proposes that "Hispalis" is Latin for "these posts," referring to posts that are supposed to have been used to strengthen the foundations of buildings in Seville's marshy terrain. During the 5th century Seville was both the capital of the Vandals and the Visigoths, when it was known as *Spalis*. The Moors arrived in 712 and renamed it *Ishbilya*. It was conquered by the Catholic Kings in 1248.

Poet Manuel Machado, born in Seville, in 1874 composed an "Ode to Andalusia." Through his words he conveys the message that no adjective is sufficient or required for his beloved hometown, as its name alone says it all.

> Cádiz, salada claridad,
> Granada, agua oculta que llora.
> Romana y mora, Córdoba callada,
> Málaga, cantaóra,
> Almería, dorada.
> Plateado Jaén.
> Huelva, la orilla de las tres caravelas.
> Y Sevilla.

> Cádiz, charming clarity,
> Granada, hidden waters that weep.
> Roman and Moorish, Córdoba silent,
> Málaga, Flamenco songstress,
> Almería, the golden.
> Silvery Jaén
> Huelva, the shore of the three caravelles (of Columbus.)
> And Seville.

Taifa: This term is derived from *ta'ifa*, meaning "section" or "party" as in a "political" party. Taifas were the regional states of al-Andalus that were formed when Islamic faith was weakening during the 11th century. Each Taifa had its own ruler, known as *al-Mûluk al-Tawâ'if*, meaning "The Party King."

Tarifa: This town, located at the southern-most point of mainland Europe where the Mediterranean meets the Atlantic, is named after Tarif ibn Malik who landed here in 710. Tarifa became part of the Christian Kingdom in 1292.

Ta'arifah, which gives us the word *tariff*, is Arabic for "price list" and a great deal of commercial traffic between Europe and Africa has been passing through here for centuries. The Spanish equivalent of *tarifa* equally means "rate" or "tariff." On the same subject, the Spanish word for "customs" is *aduana*, a term derived from its Arabic equivalent, *al-diwan*.

Toledo: The name of this town just over 40 miles south of Madrid comes from the Romans who named it *Toletum*, meaning "raised high." Toledo became the capital of the Visigoths; however few remnants of their culture remain unless you take into consideration the foundations they laid which remain in place under the city's marvelous architecture. When the Moors arrived, they named the town *Tulaytulah.*

In 1085, Alfonso VI and El Cid brought the Reconquest to Toledo and not only did Toledo become the capital of the Kingdom of Castile, but it also became the intellectual center of Christian Europe. It was in Toledo that the king and queen of Spain established the Inquisition in 1485. The town is composed of winding mazes of alleyways up and down hill that can only be explored on foot. It is a spectacular historic city that hasn't changed much since medieval times and is declared a World Heritage Site by UNESCO.

Úbeda: This picturesque and historical town in the province of Jaén derives its name from *Ubbadat al-Arab*; it was named by its founder Abd al-Rahman II. Under the Roman Empire it was known as *Bétula* for its location near the Guadalquivir River, that was then known as *Baetis.*

Zabazoque (Thaba-thokeh): This title is derived from *as-sahib as-suq*, meaning "the leader of the market" or "the lord of the zoco." However, as of the 11th century, the market inspector was known as *al-muhstasib* (as described in the beginning of this chapter).

Zambra (Thambra): There are many versions of the origins of this term. The word *Zambra*, according to the book *Rebelión y Castigo de los Moriscos* by *Luis del Mármol Carvajal*, is Arabic and designates a band of musicians as well as the festivals at which they played and sang. According to the dictionary of the *Real Academia Española*, it is derived from the Arabic *samra*, a nocturnal party, a spontaneous celebration with dance and music, or an evening celebration that lasts all night. The *Diccionario Moderno, Langenscheidt* defines it as "an uproar, a row." In the *Diccionario Flamenco de Jose Blas Vega y Manuel Rios Ruiz*, Zambra is defined as the sounds of certain instruments and confusing and cluttered voices. In *Collins Spanish-English Dictionary*, it is defined as a Moorish feast, festival, merry-making, and noisy stir.

It appears that the Mozárabes used the term *zamr* to describe their celebrations and dances. It has been written that in these festivities, plenty of wine was consumed and there was a great frolic of music and dancing. Some believe that it is derived from *zamr* (noisy) and others insist that this is the Arabic translation of "flute" or "joy." In either case, "Zambra" eventually became an Arabic synonym for a "celebration" or "party" and may also be related to *zamara* (musicians or music), that is the plural form of *zamir* (musician). It has also been linked to *samira*, meaning "entertainment" or "lively female companion/ conversationalist of the evening."

The term is also used to describe a theatrical song and music style of Flamenco that is accompanied by a full orchestra; this became popular during the 1940s and 1950s. Stories and poetic verses in the form of Flamenco song were recited with gestures, postures, and great enthusiasm. The most famous were those made popular by Manolo Caracol and Lola Flores, who took their Zambras on tour throughout Spain between 1944 and 1951. Some of the best Zambras of this type were composed by Quintero, León, and Quiroga, such as *La Niña de Fuego* and *La Salvaora*.

Zaragoza (Thara-gotha): This is the name of a town located on the Ebro River whose origins goes back to the days of the Romans, who named it after its founder, "Caesarea Augusta." The Moors, who conquered Zaragoza in 713, pronounced it as *Sarakosta*. The town was conquered by Alfonso I of Aragón in 1118, who established Zaragoza as the capital of his kingdom.

Zoco (Tho-ko): is the Spanish word for "bazaar" or "market," where craftsmen and merchants sell their goods. This term is derived from the Arabic, *sûq*. The term or name "Zacatín" referring to a clothes market within a village square is derived from *saqqatin*, meaning "clothes sellers."

As you have seen by now, the letters "s" and "z" are often pronounced with a "th" sound as in the word "thick." I have often been asked why and if the story of the Spanish King who lisped was true — the story goes that King Fernando spoke with a lisp, and that his people either felt sorry for him or thought they could ingratiate themselves by speaking as he did, and

therefore they adopted a lisp in their speech. This is merely an annoying urban legend that has been told and retold many times by non-Spaniards. This
so-called "lisp" does not appear in any other Spanish speaking country in
the world, and in Spain it is more pronounced in the region of Andalusia.
I remember being amused by a taxi driver on my way to the train station
in Granada who affirmatively replied to a question with, *"thi theñora!"* This
pronunciation is not a lisp; it is simply a local difference in pronunciation,
and distinguishes people of this region from those of other Spanish-speaking
regions in the world.

10. Paella

The traditional dish of Spain, paella (pronounced pa-eh-ya) is a colorful mixture of delicious rice, vegetables, chicken, and seafood. It is prepared and served in a round, flat bottomed, two-handled metal known as a *paellera* (pa-eh-yera). Believed to have been introduced to Spain by the Romans, the name is derived from the Latin *patella* meaning "pan" or "pot."

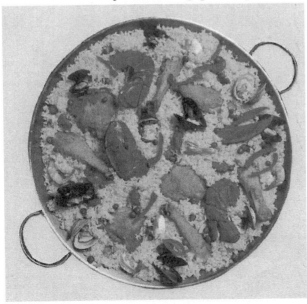

A tasty paella

Others believe that the origin of the word "paella" comes from the Arabic *baqiyah*, meaning "leftovers." This goes back to the late 8th century, when rice and its cultivation were introduced to Spain by the Moors. Household servants would take home the rice, chicken, and vegetables that their employers left at the end of the meal. Also people of modest means would inevitably make their afternoon meals of whatever sensible ingredients they could add to their rice. All these foods were combined and consumed as one dish, which eventually evolved into the various styles of paella.

Rice, introduced to Spain by the Moors, is known as *arroz*, derived from the Arabic *ar-ruzz*. Round, medium-short grain rice is best as it has just the right starch content to achieve the desired texture in paellas. The (olive) oil in which the vegetables are sautéed is known as *aceite*, derived from its Arabic equivalent of *az-zayt*. More olive oil is produced in Andalusia than anywhere else in the world. Saffron, introduced to Spain by the Moors during the 10th century, is known as *azafrán*, derived from the Arabic *za'afaran* (a derivative of *asfar* or *safra*, meaning "yellow"). It is this precious spice that gives the paella its bright yellow color and unique flavor. Ancient Sumerian texts reveal that saffron, with its proven healing properties, has been in use for over 5,000 years since it was first cultivated in Mesopotamia. During Roman times, this spice with its unique scent was also used to perfume bath water.

Today Spain and Iran are the major producers of fine quality saffron; however, it is also cultivated in India, Morocco, and Greece. It is generally agreed that the finest saffron comes from the region known as *Castilla La Mancha* that includes Albacete, Cuenca, and Toledo. This spice is also cultivated in Murcia and Valencia. The production of saffron is quite intensive as the flowers are picked by hand. It takes over 75,000 blossoms to produce a single pound, making it the most precious spice in the world. Fortunately, due to its powerful coloring qualities, very little is needed to produce a spectacular effect.

Traditionally, the paella was prepared outdoors, in the countryside over a fast-burning wood fire, for a Sunday lunch or picnic. Valencia is the home of the paella and from here the dish quickly spread throughout the country. Several variations are available within the provinces but they remain essentially similar, never steering too far away from the original recipe. Today there many varieties to choose from including paellas with rabbit, lobster, mussels, crabs, and sausages. From the menus throughout Spain, you can select from Paella Valenciana (chicken without seafood), Paella Mixta (chicken, seafood, and rabbit), Paella Verdura (vegetables), Paella Marisco (seafood) or the Paella Negra (black) — when it is flavored (and colored) with the black ink of squid.

PAELLA RECIPE

The metal paella pans used in Spain are available in many sizes. However, if you do not have access to one, a medium electric or regular 12" to 14" frying pan, skillet or casserole can be used. Remember that the heat source must be large enough to accommodate the size of the pan. This is my mother's recipe; it takes one hour to prepare and serves four.

2 lbs diced uncooked chicken
2 Cups uncooked long or traditional short grain rice
5 Cups boiling water or chicken stock
6 Tablespoons of olive oil
1 medium onion
3 cloves garlic , chopped
2 large bay leaves
1 red and yellow pepper, diced
2 medium tomatoes, peeled and chopped
½ Cup peas
1/8 teaspoon saffron
1 medium carrot, raw, diced
2 lbs of seafood; shrimp, clams, scampi or *calamari* (squid)
1 medium-sized Spanish sausage or *chorizo*
1 lemon, cut in wedges
Salt to taste

In the heated oil sauté onion, garlic, peppers and carrots for five minutes.
Add tomatoes and bay leaf and cook for five more minutes.
Add chicken and rice and cook for five more minutes.
Add boiling water, peas, saffron and salt, simmer uncovered for 20 minutes.

Remove from heat, let it stand for a few minutes, add seafood and sausage, and garnish with lemon wedges.

Valencia is not only known for having the best paellas but for being the largest rice growing region in the country. It is also well known for holding

La Fiesta de la Tomatina or the annual tomato throwing festival usually held on the last Wednesday of every August.

The origins of this tradition go back to 1945 when a few men began a tomato fight in the town square of the village of Buñol, about 25 miles from the capital city of Valencia, during a festival. The tomato-throwing is said to have started as a protest against the town council for not allowing another festival to take place. *La Tomatina* was officially banned, until 1959, and it especially grew in popularity during the 1980s. Since then, thousands of locals and foreign tourists join in the chaotic fun of throwing ripe tomatoes at each other, leaving everyone completely drenched in its juice. The event lasts for one hour, ending at noon, attracting spectators from all around the world.

For this extravaganza, 120 tons of the red fruit are brought in by truck loads annually and it literally becomes "the war of the tomatoes." La Tomatina is actually just one of the activities that take place during the week-long celebrations of fireworks, music, dance, food, and other on-going festivities. The festival grows bigger and attracts more participants each year. The one in August 2006 cost 36,000 Euros and drew over 40,000 participants.

Although rice has been cultivated in Spain for over a thousand years, the potato, another favorite, did not appear in Europe until the 16th century. It was from Spain however, that the potato gradually spread throughout Europe after it was introduced by Spanish conquistadors who brought it back home from their expeditions into South America. Originally known as *papas*, the conquistadores named in *patata* and in Andalusia, potatoes are still referred to as "papas."

Today, the potato is the main ingredient of two delicious dishes that are served throughout every region of Spain as well as in every home and bar as an appetizer or meal; *Tortilla de Patata* or *Tortilla Española* (Potato or Spanish Omelet) and *Ensaladilla Rusa* (Russian Salad or Spanish Potato Salad.)

We have arrived at the end of my research and will close this final chapter with a word on *tapas*. Tapas are the Andalusian tradition of consuming small portions of food with an alcoholic beverage, such as wine, in between the main meals. These appetizers have become traditional and, as with all traditions, there are several versions of both its origins and name.

The word actually means "cover" or "lid," and the least romantic theory holds that the glass was covered in order to keep flies away. Another theory goes back to the 13th century when King Alfonso X became ill and could only consume small quantities of food and wine; he was advised to take small snacks between meals along with some wine. As he recovered, he ordered all inns to serve drinks accompanied with small amounts of food.

The most widely accepted theory is that in the taverns of long ago, a piece of bread or ham on a plate was placed on top of the wine glass in order to minimize the effects of alcohol consumed on an empty stomach. Later, in the 16th century, King Felipe II actually passed a royal decree requiring tavern keepers to serve a small amount of food with each glass of wine or sherry served in order to reduce public inebriation. One way or the other, it has become a tavern keepers' tradition to serve tapas with drinks. The idea has recently developed into a concept called *tapear*, or bar-hopping, going from one bar or tavern to another, sampling drinks and sharing tapas with friends. Tapear has become an integral part of everyday social life in Spain.

References

Aulestia, Gorka, et al. *Basque-English, English-Basque Dictionary.* Nevada, US; University of Nevada Press, 1992.

Aznar, Fernando. *España Medieval; Musulmanes, Judios y Cristianos.* Madrid, Spain; Grupo Anaya, S.A., 1990

Borrow, George. *The Zincalí or an Account of the Gypsies of Spain.* London, UK; John Murray Publishing, 1846.

Brisset Martín, Demetrio E. *Las Fiestas del la Granada Musulmana.* Granada, Spain; Gazeta de Antropología, No 5, 1987.

Cadalso, José. *Cartas Marruecas;* Barcelona, Spain; Salvat Editores S.A., 1970.

Capilla, Susana Calvo. *Urbanismo en La Córdoba Islámica.* Madrid, Spain; Edilupa Ediciones, S.L., 2002.

Casares Rodicio, Emilio. *Diccionario de la Música Española e Hispano Americana.* Madrid, Spain; Sociedad General de Autores y Editores, 1999.

Crow, John A. *The Root and the Flower.* Los Angeles, US; University of California Press, Ltd., 1963.

Díaz, José Simón. *Guía Literaria de Madrid; De Murallas Adentro.* Madrid, Spain, Ediciones La Librería, 1993.

Diccionario Enciclopedico Ilustrado del Flamenco. Madrid, Spain: Cinterco, 1988.

Edwards, Gwynne. *¡Flamenco!* London, UK; Thames and Hudson, 2000.

Fernández Manzano, Reynado. *Las Zambra de Los Morisco del Reino de Granada;* El Folklore Andaluz, Revista de Cultura Tradicional, Num. 7, 1991.

Fierro, Maribel. *Al-Andalus: saberes e intercambios culturales.* Barcelona, Spain; Icaria Editorial, S.A., 2001.

Fletcher, Richard. *Moorish Spain.* New York, US; Henry Holt and Company, Inc., 1992.

García, Juan Guirao, Ginés Pérez de Hita y Las Fiestas Moriscas de Purchena.

García, J.L. Navarro. *Cantes y Bailes de Granada*. Malaga, Spain; Editorial Arquval, 1993.

García de Cortázar. *Historia de España*. Barcelona, Spain; Editorial Planeta, S.A., 2003.

Garfias, Francisco. *Gruta de las Maravillas*. Madrid, Spain; Selecciones del Reader's Digest Iberia S.A., 1980.

Grupo SP et al. *Flamenco*. Madrid; Biblioteca Multimedia de la Cultura.

Guardia, José. *La Opera Flamenca en Granada*. Granada, Spain; Editorial Comares, 1997.

Harvey, L.P. *Islamic Spain 1250 to 1500*. Chicago, US; University of Chicago Press, 1990.

Irving, Washington. *The Alhambra; a Series of Tales and Sketches of the Moors and Spaniards*. London, UK; Messrs. Colburn and Bentley of London, 1832.

Matteo. *The Language of Spanish Dance*. New Jersey, US; Princeton Book Company, Publishers, 1990.

Mederos, Alicia. *El Flamenco*. Madrid, Spain; Acento Editorial, 1996.

Nicolle, David. *The Moors; The Islamic West 7th-15th Centuries AD*. Oxford, UK; Osprey Publishing, 2001.

Reilly, Bernard F. *The Medieval Spains*. Cambridge, UK; Cambridge University Press, 1993.

Rodriguez-Valdes, Angel. *Flamenco Orígenes y Misterios*. Seville, Spain; Promociones Al-Andalus, S.L., 1998.

Romera, José Joaquín Sandoval. *La Música de los Moriscos*. 2001.

Ruiz, Joaquina Albarracín. *Vestido y Adorno de la Mujer Musulmana de Yebala (Marruecos)*. Madrid, Spain; Consejo Superior de Investigaciones Científicas, 1964.

Schreiner, Claus, et al. *Flamenco*. Oregon, US; Amadeus Press, 1990.

Spence, Lewis. *España; Mitos y Leyendas*. Madrid, Spain; M.E. Editores, S.L., 1995.

Vallvé, J. et al. *Los árabes invaden España*. Madrid, Spain; Grupo 16, 1985.

Vilchez, Carlos Vilchez. *Baños Arabes*. Granada; Diputación de Granada Sección de Publicaciones, 2001.

Viñegla, José L. Alonso. *Al-Hamar; Perfil Biográfico de un Caballero Andalusí*. Jaén, Spain; Colección Icaro, 1990.

Watt, W. Montgomery. *Historia de la España islámica*. Madrid, Spain; Alianza Editorial, S.A., 1970.

Weiditz, Cristoph. *Das Trachtenbuch des Christoph Weiditz von sienen Reisen nach Spanien (1529) und Niederlanden (1531/32)*. Berlin and Leipzig, Germany; Walter de Gruyter & Co., 1927.

Index

1089850R0

Printed in Great Britain by
Amazon.co.uk, Ltd.,
Marston Gate.